Midnight's Gate

午
夜
之
門

For dear Jane & Mel
with best wishes

北島
Bei Dao
April 14, 2006

RAINMAKER TRANSLATIONS supports a series of books meant to encourage a lively reading experience of contemporary world literature drawn from diverse languages and cultures. Publication is assisted by grants from the International Institute of Modern Letters (modernletters.org), a nonprofit organization dedicated to promoting the literary arts and literary activism around the world.

Bei Dao

Midnight's Gate

Translated from the Chinese by MATTHEW FRYSLIE
Edited by CHRISTOPHER MATTISON

A New Directions Book

Some of these essays first appeared in *Positions*, *Turnrow*, and *World Literature Today*.

Grateful acknowledgments: Excerpt by Marcel Proust in "Paris Stories" is from *Swann's Way*, translated by Lydia Davis (Penguin Books, Reprint edition 2004). The poems by Li Po and Wang Wei in "Empty Mountain" are from *The Selected Poems of Li Po* (New Directions, 1996) and *Mountain Home: The Wilderness Poetry of Ancient China* (New Directions, 2005), translated by David Hinton. Excerpts by Harald Salfellner in "Kafka's Prague" are from *Franz Kafka and Prague* (Vitalis Prague, Third Edition, 1998). Excerpts from *The True Confessions of an Albino Terrorist* by Breyten Breytenbach, copyright © 1984 by Breyten Breytenbach; reprinted by permission of Farrar, Straus and Giroux, LLC. The fragment of Federico García Lorca's "Somnambule Ballad" in "The Master of Ithaca" is translated by Stephen Spender and J. L. Gili, from *The Selected Poetry of Federico García Lorca*, edited by Donald M. Allen (New Directions, 1955).

Manufactured in the United States of America
New Directions Books are printed on acid-free paper.
First published as a New Directions Paperbook (NDP1008) in 2005.
Published simultaneously in Canada by Penguin Books Canada Limited

Library of Congress Cataloging-in-Publication Data
Bei Dao, 1949–
[Wu ye shi men. English]
Midnight's gate / Bei Dao ; Translated from the Chinese
by Matthew Fryslie ;
Edited by Christopher Mattison.
    p. cm.
ISBN 0-8112-1584-9 (alk. paper)
1. Bei Dao, 1949–Translations into English. I. Fryslie, Matthew.
II. Title.
PL2892.E525W8213   2005
895.1′352–dc22   2004028185

New Directions Books are published for James Laughlin
by New Directions Publishing Corporation
80 Eighth Avenue, New York, NY 10011

For Qi and Tiantian

Table of Contents

Midnight's Gate

午夜之門

I

NEW YORK VARIATIONS

I

I MOVED TO NEW YORK because of a conflagration. Of course, conflagration is merely a figurative way of referring to a certain extraordinary state of affairs, which in my case was a revolution. On my second day in New York, I woke up at four in the morning. Looking out my nineteenth-floor window, New York seemed to be on fire, its skyscrapers all in flames, thousands upon thousands of glass shards glinting bloody red, black birds wheeling into the sky—a truly apocalyptic scene. As it turned out, my alarm clock was still running on California time; day was just breaking in New York.

Then that night, it was New York's moon that startled me. Wedged between two tall buildings, the moon was enormous and bright, but no matter how I gazed at it, something didn't look quite right. If you ask a child from New York to draw the moon, most of their creations would not be round, but staggered and misshapen, clipped by glass and concrete.

In 1626, a Dutch superintendent purchased Manhattan—this thirty-mile long, two and a half-mile wide island of stone—from the Indians with trinkets worth about twenty-four dollars. In the nineteenth century, due to the widespread use of reinforced concrete, people madly spread upward into the sky, until one day New Yorkers discovered that they were nesting like birds in a concrete forest.

New Yorkers are unable to imagine the horizon, a concept that from birth has no relevance to them. If in California my thinking was horizontal, here it certainly became vertical. When the elevator brought me from the ground to the nineteenth floor, my thoughts followed the inertia of upward motion, continuing to rise into the blue of the sky. In proportion to its population, few New Yorkers are religious. After some consideration, I have come to the conclusion that this has something to do with the elevators. When you spend the entire day ascending into the sky and then plunging down through the earth, it is almost impossible to have any sense of the mysteries of heaven or the underworld. In one sense, the elevator has become the *primum mobile* of New Yorkers' thinking. If the electricity should go out, they would be trapped somewhere in the middle, and might certainly go mad.

On my second day in New York, I wandered the streets, taking note of all the people. In addition to the vertical orientation of their thinking are certain linear qualities. For example, they are never vague when making appointments: 23rd Street and Seventh Avenue, or between Wall Street and Broadway. Later I began to understand that they are all just pieces on a chessboard. Their paths are mostly fixed, and the hands that pluck them up and move them are money, fate, and linear logic. But this doesn't mean that New Yorkers are only capable of shuttling back and forth in straight lines: opposed to the geography and plan of the streets are the labyrinths of their hearts and winding coils of their guts. It is the twists and turns of power and the curves of the stock market that creates these convolutions in the souls of New Yorkers.

2

THE FIRST TIME I VISITED New York was in the summer of 1988. I flew in from London. Compared to the moribund British Empire, this place had a kind of heedless power. In Beijing, people call this sort of reckless and impulsive atmosphere *lengtou qing* (literally "crude green"). When I first got off the plane, my cousin's boyfriend took us for a drive. We looked back at the buildings of Manhattan from across the East River. It was twilight, and the lights were all ablaze. On the second day, I rode the subway into the city, and nearly passed out from the stench of urine before I was finally able, ashen and shaken, to crawl back out to the surface. When I looked up, the filthy skyscrapers pressed down on me so hard that I had to gasp for breath. Fortunately, they block the sun on the most sweltering of days.

We went to the East Village to look for W. Years earlier, when my first collection of poems was printed on a mimeograph machine, W had drawn the cover art. I had met my ex-wife, Shao Fei, through him. W first came to the U.S. in the '80s and had been living illegally in New York for seven or eight years. People have different reactions to living illegally. Some people live as if they're walking on thin ice, while others take to it like a fish to water. New York remakes people like no other place. This man who was a good student—a sophomore in film school, majoring in animation—had completely transformed himself. His eyes were gloomy, his face fatter, and his ears bigger. Dressed in shorts, he was now full of New York slang. As he walked down the street all sorts of people walked over to greet him, their faces full of respect. At that time, the East Village was a land of the homeless, drunks, drug dealers, and those suffering from AIDS. He would always grunt a response, but would not say much, just pat them on the shoulder, or stroke their bald heads, and miraculously, their enraged, crazy spirits would calm instantly.

He told us that in two day's time, this brotherhood of the poor and suffering was going to hold a demonstration in Washington Square to protest the city government's decision to chase out the homeless, and that the police would certainly squash it. Because of this, he had spent a considerable sum on a repeating flash for his camera. When the mounted police charged into the ranks of the demonstrators, at the moment the police raised their nightsticks, he snapped photos. They were published in local papers. TV news crews also reported from the scene of the demonstration. As an eyewitness, he related the details of the police violence. Even though shots of his face were blocked out for the broadcast, it still made him sweat because he was an illegal immigrant. If the police ever found out they would certainly retaliate.

I asked him how he made a living, and he said he painted people's portraits on the street. He then got out his painting tools, hailed a taxi, and dragged us to a prosperous section of West Fourth Street, where a number of other Chinese painters were already trying to drum up business. Unfortunately, luck was not with him that evening as he waited two hours with no one even inquiring about prices. When someone suggested he go to Atlantic City for a little gambling, he immediately closed up shop and sailed off.

W was a buddy of Allen Ginsberg's. Allen would announce his name with great exaggeration. When I first came to New York, Allen invited us to dinner at a Japanese restaurant, and W went along to translate. He ridiculed Allen in Chinese. Allen stared at him and smiled wickedly, seeming to understand everything. He told Allen about the police suppression of the demonstration, and Allen immediately made a public state-ment. In New York, one can find almost every type of under-ground society; and the fact that W was happy to enter the ranks of those on the margins of society and fight for justice shows that he was born to rebel. This must be the main reason that, many years ago, he joined the Xingxing Painters' Club.

Later, I heard W had returned to China where he made a fortune as a major antiques dealer in Beijing. It wasn't that surprising as commercialism digests everything in the end. Besides, the antiques business is an underground society; the courage and insight he had won from his struggles in New York proved enough.

3

MICHAEL IS A NEW YORKER, but now lives in Prague. Two days ago he came to New York on business. After graduating with a degree in history from Columbia—treading in the foot-steps of Pound and Eliot—he moved to London where he married and had children, and was trapped for more than twenty years. A few years ago, released from his familial re-sponsibilities, he moved to Prague to work for The Prague International Writers' Festival. The festival wanted to invite Arthur Miller to serve as its chairman, and Michael needed to attend to the matter in person. So with financial assistance from *The Guardian*, the Prague city government, DHL, a cell phone provided by GlobalOne, and a plane ticket donated by Swissair, the ex-New Yorker was packed up and sent back to his old hometown.

Michael asked me to reserve a hotel room for him. I looked everywhere, but he was on a limited budget, so all I could come up with was a B&B in Greenwich Village.

After I moved to New York, Michael once told me over the phone, "The place you are living in is just two or three blocks from the place I was born. You should go and take a look." The doorbell rang, and Michael walked in wearing his trademark smile. He had brought six small wineglasses of pink crystal for me, as well as the brochure for the year's writers' festival. On the cover was a semiabstract oil painting by a Czech artist, composed of circles of varying sizes. All of them were graves. Michael sighed and then pointed to a little circle in the back row and said, "That one's mine."

A few days later, I emerged from the subway station in the afternoon as we had arranged to meet up to talk before visiting another friend together. Michael appeared in the drizzle, wearing a black woolen coat, his thinning hair uncombed. "Look! This is my New York," he said, both arms outstretched. But the truth was that this had not been his New York for a long time. He was being sentimental, feeling nostalgic about everything that had passed away. But real New Yorkers eschew such warm feelings; they are daily witnesses to life's cruelties. He said that the B&B wasn't bad, and the owner was quite friendly. The only drawback was that his room had no windows. I imagined him sitting alone, facing the wall in the darkness, while beyond it New York exploded in lights.

We sat in a coffee shop. The place was decorated in a reserved antique elegance that was painstaking without being obsessive. Most of the customers seemed to be locals. A college student was doing her homework at a side table. "New York has changed. New Yorkers never used to talk about money," Michael said, sipping a cup of strong coffee with his eyes closed. "Now everything is so blatant." He told me that he had no family left in New York, and that he no longer even spoke to his stepfather in Miami. After his mother's death, he wrote to his stepfather simply to ask for a clock that his mother had liked, as a memento. But instead, his stepfather sold the clock and sent Michael some money to buy a new clock.

I bought one of the coffee shop's T-shirts for his girl-friend, and wrote a few words to her on a Marilyn Monroe postcard. Heading out the door, I couldn't repress a shiver. A New Yorker who relieves his homesickness with tears, drifting from one place to another without even a souvenir to represent his past, and then, returning home at last, ends up staying in a windowless room.

4

NEW YORK TAXIS SEEM TO be reserved for our brothers from poor and war-torn places, and many of them drive as though they are still fighting battles in their minds. One day, during the war in Kosovo, my taxi driver was a Serb who had just come from the front lines. Without warning, he arched his back and turned the steering wheel at top speed, weaving and dodging, clearly still trying to avoid gunfire. His eyes were locked straight ahead, his expression both anxious and exultant. Perhaps it was the feeling of going deep behind enemy lines—plunging right into the heart of American imperialism.

The goals of some taxi drivers are very concrete. On one ride, my driver was a middle-aged peasant from the ravines of

Turkey. I could see his melancholy eyes in the rear-view mirror. His greatest wish was to make enough money to buy a good car and go back home in style. He asked me in detail about the features and prices of each make of car, unable to have the best yet unwilling to settle for less, talking to me as if I managed a car lot. Fortunately, I love cars myself, and took the opportunity to show off my little knowledge in this area. He covertly fingered a small abacus and reached the conclusion that he could go home the following year. He hated New York. Through clenched teeth, he said it was hell.

I have an American friend who is an old New York hand. Once, while taking a taxi to JFK, he casually asked the driver where he was from. The driver immediately took offense and said, in a very thick foreign accent, "Where are you from where are you from, everybody always asks, but then when I tell them my country, nobody knows it." My friend asked if he could try. The driver agreed and said that he would name the country and if my friend could name the capital the ride was free, otherwise he'd double the fare. My friend agreed. The driver said Albania. My friend not only knew Tirana, but he also mentioned the name of a famous Albanian tenor, which pleased the driver to no end, and when he got out of the cab, the driver refused to take any money.

Two days ago on my way to the dress rehearsal of a small theatrical troupe near Washington Square, I hailed a cab. The driver was very distinguished in his appearance, like a Hamlet who was just about to leave the political stage. His name was Louis, he was a dramatic actor, and he had been part of the backbone of the street theater that thrived in New York in the sixties and seventies. He had always had a strong fondness for China. His father had been second in command of a unit in the American "Flying Tigers" during the war against Japan, but he did not allow him to travel in China. When we talked about the presidential election, he said that Bush was a moron and represented the interests of American arms dealers. On the subject of rent in New York, he called the mayor the boss of a crime syndicate composed of three types of people: lawyers, bankers, and developers. We exchanged phone numbers. As I was getting out of the car, he told me that when the tide of revolution ebbed, and he discovered that there was no place for him in society, driving a taxi and playing the occasional bit part was the only thing he could do. He said, "You haven't woken up, man. The world has fucking changed."

5

MY DAUGHTER, TIANTIAN, doesn't like New York. Not long ago she came here to visit me for a couple weeks. For a child who has grown up in Beijing, then lived for five years in a small town in rural California—from fifth grade through middle school—and then returned to Beijing last summer for high school, one can imagine that this is a confusing experience. Living in California, she missed Beijing, but then she was disappointed after she moved back to Beijing. She is not one to forget her friends. She misses her California classmates, but she doesn't like the United States, and in the future, she wants to move to a new country she knows nothing about. Sixteen is a depressing age, and what with migrating from country to country, cultural shifts, domestic turmoil, and the restlessness of youth added in, one must be careful of everything.

Tiantian slept on the sofa in the living room. Maybe because of jet lag or her rejection of New York, she refused to wake up in the morning; and she would have absolutely no energy until late in the evening when she would bounce all over the room, making me dizzy. On top of a cabinet in the living room was an old clock that quit working many years ago, its parts rusted together. Tiantian never wore a watch, but in an attempt to create some reference between New York and Beijing time, when she had nothing else to do, she would pound on the rusted clock, move the hands, and swing the pendulum. It never worked for very long.

When you visit New York, you have to go someplace high up. I offered to take Tiantian to the Empire State Building. "Why the Empire State Building?" she asked. "It's tall." "Taller than a mountain?" This stopped me in my tracks. "All right, then. Let's go to Central Park." "Why Central Park?" "It's big." "How big?" I wasted some time trying to show her with gestures, and finally dug out a map of New York. "That speck?" she spat out disdainfully, "Forget it." In the end, we took a walk through SoHo. As soon as we stepped into a clothing store for young people, I became an embarrassment to her. She quickly told me where and when to meet her later, dismissing me with a few words.

We took Tiantian to Auntie Q's house for a visit. Auntie Q's husband, Peter, was a German Jew. His entire family had died in the Nazi concentration camps; he was the only one who had escaped. Peter used to be a psychiatrist in New York for many years, but every week he spent money to go see a psychiatrist himself. They lived in a modern apartment building downtown, on the Lower East Side. On entering its doors, we saw ourselves reflected in the shiny marble, and doormen dressed like generals. It was easy to get lost among the mirrors. Their home was immaculate, with a snow-white sofa and snow-white carpet; spotlights cast light on various oil paintings.

"Just like a five-star hotel," said Tiantian, sticking her tongue out in surprise.

Auntie Q made us a full meal of authentic Shanghai food. Peter had a large forehead, like the god of longevity. He could, in the most peculiar accent, speak several phrases of Chinese, such as *la guanxi* ("pull strings") or he mocked himself saying *dacuo le jin* ("I've popped a spring or two"). We had brought two bottles of red wine that we drank with great trepidation, fearing that a drop might fall on the white carpet beneath our feet. After dinner, Peter took out photos from their most recent trip to China. Before looking at them, he warned Tiantian that he had a "condition" and that she could only look at the photo album if she wore rubber gloves. When I gave Tiantian the photo album, she reached out one hand, and at the same time, she held out a rubber glove as a make-believe hand and waved at me.

6

G HAD A COMMON HAN CHINESE surname, but since his ancestors were Manchu bannermen of the Plain Yellow Banner, and had protected the dynastic succession, he wanted to change his back to the imperial surname of Nala. The story that a member of his family had been Director of Defense Districts during the last two generations was believable. If one went back several more generations, I would guess that most of his relatives probably attacked city walls—nomadic pastoralists who lived wherever there was water and grass.

Otherwise, how could they have raced so quickly to Holland from Beijing, and then from Holland battled their way to the U.S., rampaging north and south. The answer must lie somewhere deep in the blood.

At the time, G was the youngest member of the Xingxing Painters' Club—eighteen years old, bright-eyed, and with a foolish grin. I remember him helping hang paintings at the Club's exhibition in Beihai Park. He didn't talk much, and kept very busy. The sunny young Beijing boy of those days had been transformed into a gloomy New Yorker when I met him again in the fall of '88. Solemnly fulfilling his hostly duties, he drove us to a beach in Connecticut, took us on a stroll around Harlem, and treated us to dinner at the Great Wall of China.

When I moved to the U.S. in 1993, I learned that while painting and making experimental movies, G had plunged into Wall Street and, with a snap of his fingers, had become a businessman. Even more odious, people said he had two wives, who soon gave birth to two daughters, differing in age by no more than a few days. I called to ask him about the rumors. He would neither confirm nor deny them. I suppose it doesn't really matter, as such things have been happening for ages. What I felt strange about was the fact that I had never sensed his madness.

After I moved to New York, we often drank together on the weekends. He liked to drink scotch, neat, with no ice. When we got a little buzzed, he would always select metaphysical topics of conversation, which he would expound in English, until he no longer made any sense. When he smiled, it was only with great effort and the results were, for the most part, incomplete and fragmented.

There were many contradictions in his character: he was

manic, yet suppressed; he felt disgust for fame and wealth, yet had a great thirst for success; he treated his friends sincerely, yet was too demanding of them; he was both violent and fragile. He had been educated in the West, but deep in his bones he was authentically Chinese. He was extremely strange, but only the truly strange can live in the forest of buildings that is New York. For the past two years, he has lived in New Jersey, staring back at Manhattan from across the river. This turned out to be a very bad move as his New Yorker's heart was gravely injured. His paintings reflected this: structures shaped as ruins appear dreamlike in the monochrome background of an endless, lonely, flat road. He started to keep fish at home, sought out only ugly and strange tropical varieties, feeding them his own heart, cultivating his light in dark secrecy.

His style of painting changed again. He now painted a batch of furious horses, eyes wild and manes blowing, as though they were his own self-portraits. I chose one as the cover for my collection *At the Sky's Edge*. I suddenly realized, in terms of our personalities, that though we had split in opposite directions there was one commonality—a fury in our hearts. In a certain sense, the sky's edge is the correlate of the mad horse. Seen in this way, our meeting in New York was not without fate.

7

EARLY ONE SATURDAY MORNING, G drove into Manhattan to pick me up. We crossed the bridge into Queens and got on Interstate 495. There is a lot of traffic on the way out to Long Island during the summer. It was already one o'clock by the

time we crawled into Water Mill. I covertly made a call on my
cell phone to leak news of our arrival. S was standing at the
end of the road, his gray hair waving like a flag.

We originally met at a press conference for the launch of
an international periodical. I had arrived an hour early, and
was wandering the halls like a lonely ghost. Someone finally
appeared, sidled over, and shook my hand. This was S.
Though I'd never met him before, I asked him to read the English translations of my poems. After the reading, we dined
together. We exchanged addresses, and he made me promise
to visit him at his house in the country. For a New Yorker, this
kind of promise is not something to be taken seriously. A
month later, he called out of the blue, "Do you remember me?
Aren't you coming out?"

Beyond the window, the sea and sky were the same color,
gulls flew in a row. S's wife, Jane, a retired sociologist, chatted
with us pleasantly. S was in his seventies. Both a poet and a
publisher, it was his art business that he lived on. He dealt
solely in classical Italian and Spanish paintings, and had dealings with every imaginable museum. I asked him if he had a
family inheritance. He shook his head and said that he'd
started from scratch. His first lessons he learned from an old
girlfriend, an Italian painter. While we talked in the living
room, the horizontal rays of the setting sun shone on his face.
He squinted, his entire face suffused with fatigue. Then there
was a long silence until the sunlight gently slid past and he
slipped into darkness.

The next day when I went downstairs, S was in the study.
He said he had been up since five o'clock, reading a book on
entomology.

A week later I received a call from him, this time there was
a dinner party at his house in Riverdale. His luxurious home

enjoyed a panoramic view of the Hudson River. Looking out
from the terrace, in the subtly changing light, the perspective
of the sky, river, and hills was distinct. His house was a miniature museum. Almost all of his paintings were Renaissance
masterpieces, along with works by Borromini and Goya.

Tonight's guests of honor were the American poet laureate Stanley Kunitz and his wife, who sat at either end of the
table. S had hired a few people to help out, but he was the
chef. Seated next to Kunitz was a female poet who was bat-
tling AIDS and who had an unfathomable look in her eyes, a
resolve to look death straight on. S and I sat on each side of
Mrs. Kunitz. She was ninety-five years old and spoke like a
child, innocently and disconnectedly. She asked someone to
put a little water in her red wine. "Now that's much better,"
she took a sip and said to me, "I can't see any of the guests
here clearly, it's only the voices I recognize."

S was very talkative that night, his conversation ranging
from the Italian character to the lives of insects. He felt that
insects had their own world, making love in the most per-
verted ways, this a kind of blessing for them, a joy that
human beings had no way of understanding. He woke up one
day to discover two bats making love on his chest. "I am
afraid of bats," said Mrs. Kunitz. S then talked about his love
of snakes. Mrs. Kunitz made a face and said, "I am afraid of
snakes."

8

THE OLD COUPLE WHO HAD gone to Florida for six month's
of sun was coming back, so we had to move out of the apart-

ment and stay with friends temporarily. It's true that the unit was roomy, but it was also unbearably ugly. The brown furniture was repulsive and awkward as if, after following the couple around for so many years, it had finally decided to stay put: two armchairs sat side by side facing the television, and the broken clock stood as a monument to retired life. The walls were hung with inexpensive mass-produced oil paintings and travel postcards, like little windows of various sizes peeking out on the floating world. We had no choice but to use bright-toned cloths, rugs, and pictures borrowed from our artist friends' houses to cover everything as much as possible.

Our unit was in a thirty-two-story apartment building on the Upper West Side. The building was largely low income housing, which is the only way people living in the building could possibly remain in Manhattan, where land is more valuable than gold. In the narrow space and the brief time of the elevator's ascent or descent, we would exchange a hello, and, at the most, two or three words about dogs, the weather, or children, then our gazes would break off.

In New York, "neighborhood" is an important concept. It reminds me of Beijing: knowing which restaurants don't water down their beer, which grocer has the best meat and freshest vegetables, which neighborhood committee has the most cunning old ladies, which coal shops sell honeycomb coal, which neighborhood police station has grain ration tickets—all of this was very clear in each Beijing neighborhood. In New York I learned which doormen were friendly, which clothing stores had the most attractive staff, which intersections had the least amount of traffic, and which shops had the greatest variety of beer at the cheapest prices.

Many of the homeless are reflections of their neighborhoods. Every time I went to the bank, the same old man opened the door for me, impeccably courteous and always ready with a kind remark. But the same demon always stood next to the door of the grocery store. If you didn't give him money, you'd get a face full of foul-mouthed curses. Fortunately, people are used to politicians and their bosses, and remain largely unfazed by him. Every evening when I passed by Broadway and Seventy-eighth, I invariably saw the same scrawny man lying on his mat by the side of the road, reading by penlight. Large bags and small bags surrounded him filled with books he had found. Such a spirit of dedication shamed me.

Whenever I went out, I basically followed one fixed route: I'd first walk to the Citibank at the corner of Broadway and Eighty-sixth to get cash, then I'd buy a paper at the newsstand next to the Citibank, follow Broadway to Eighty-third Street and turn left, cross the intersection to the post office. Then I'd buy a bunch of flowers on the corner, and head up Amsterdam Avenue, stop for groceries on Eighty-fifth Street, then at the liquor store next door pick up a couple bottles of red wine, and finally pass the red brick church on my way home. When it was windy or rainy, I'd take cover on the other side of the street beneath the scaffolding.

9

WE EVENTUALLY MOVED TO THE West Village. E and his family live in a typical New York row house, with its own entrance and yard. The creaking stairs connect three floors and a basement, and the backyard is narrow with a waving bamboo grove. Built in 1929, it is the oldest house on the street. It used to be divided into forty dovecote-like lodging rooms, but it had been completely remodeled by several successive owners. E and his wife had bought it ten years earlier and molded it to their personal taste.

The first thing E did when he got up every morning was fill the plastic bird feeder, then hang it back up in its fork in the tree where pigeons and sparrows would already be tumbling over each other, eager for their turn. Next he'd make coffee and read the *New York Times*—a bolt of lightning couldn't disturb him. Then the soprano who lived next door would begin to sing with the sparrows. Her voice was startling, scales climbing like a ladder into the sky.

When the Dutch first bought Manhattan Island, it was a stretch of forested land where birds flew and beasts roamed. After the English occupied it, the admiral of the English fleet bought three hundred acres of land for growing tobacco and settled down by the Hudson River. Before he died, he named his manor "Greenwich." In 1822, during a plague, people moved there for the fresh air, and this remote hamlet gradually became a prosperous town. At the end of the nineteenth century, the rich, in their pursuit of fashion, moved to the newly burgeoning uptown, and the roadside Greenwich was forgotten and went into decline. Then the artists and rebels moved in, their bohemian lifestyle and heterodox ideas shocking the religious Italian and Irish immigrants who lived there.

One day in 1916, a bunch of young men who had been drinking in a bar all night climbed to the top of the arched gate of Washington Square and announced, with much shouting and hoopla, the establishment of an independent republic—New Bohemia. They refused to come down until the mayor agreed to their request. Greenwich Village, or "Little Bohemia," enjoyed nationwide fame.

One day around noon, E came down from his study on the top floor. I asked him how the writing was going and he told me a story about Flaubert. One day at lunchtime, Flaubert came out of his study and a guest asked the same question. He replied that he had only written a comma. At dinnertime, the guest asked again, and Flaubert replied that he had crossed the comma out.

10

ON MARCH 6, 1970, THERE was an explosion at 18 West Eleventh street in the West Village. Three members of the Weather Underground had accidentally detonated a bomb that they were making and were killed on the spot. Two women survived the mishap, and ran naked to the home of their neighbor, the movie star Dustin Hoffman. They borrowed some clothes from his wife, fled to the subway, and lived on the run for two years. One later turned herself in and was dealt with leniently; the other joined the activities of another underground organization and, when finally caught, was punished severely.

The Weather Underground's precursor was the national organization, Students for a Democratic Society (SDS), established in 1960. It came to maturity in the wake of the demonstrations of the civil rights and anti-war protests, inclining more and more toward violent action. In 1969, due to diverging points of view, it split into a number of groups, one of which was the radical Weather Underground. The members of this group were mostly Columbia University students. They were radical Maoists who advocated that the flames of American imperialism be extinguished through armed revolution.

E told me that he had a classmate who was a member of the Weather Underground. Later he became an English professor. In their view, private ownership was the root of all evil, and even clothing could lead to notions of personal possession. They took off all their clothes when they entered their house, putting them in a big cardboard box, and when they went out again, they put on whatever items were at hand. Because the gender issues of the term "weathermen" conflicted with the women's liberation movement, they called themselves the Weather Underground.

From its establishment in 1969, members of the Weather Underground were arrested and taken to court many times. On June 9, 1970, three months after the West Village incident, the New York police department was bombed; on July 27, the New York offices of Bank of America were bombed, and the Weather Underground released a statement to the press claiming responsibility.

May should be when green things flourish, but the weather swung from warm back to cold again. I had a date to meet a friend from Germany for a walk around Greenwich Village. There was a misty drizzle as we followed the narrow, winding streets to the White Horse Tavern where Dylan Thomas had his last drink, then we stopped at the world's first gay bookstore, where, this weekend, we had to wait until noon for it to open. We eventually reached Washington Square. In the northwest corner were a few tables with inlaid chessboards, most of them empty. An old man who had set up a chessboard with a timer was awaiting the arrival of his opponent. We crossed the square, walked down Sixth Avenue, turned onto West Eleventh, and finally arrived at number 18.

This modern, triangular structure was rebuilt in 1978, sandwiched between two older buildings apparently with the intention of creating a certain dissonance. It was an ordinary Saturday morning. A father was standing in the doorway, kidding around with his young son; another member of the family was welcoming, or seeing off, a guest. Does anyone still remember the explosion thirty-one years ago? The Weathermen who died are forever young, but the ones who lived would be about my age and would bear the scars of the rebellious movements of the sixties. But the wind has been blowing in a different direction for a long time now. As Bob Dylan sang, "You don't need a weatherman to know which way the wind blows."

II

ON JULY 13, 1974, AN OIL tanker docked at a pier on the Delaware River. The novice sailor X and some of his shipmates took a taxi to a small town nearby, then paid the driver one hundred and fifty dollars to switch to his own car and drive them all the way to New York. Sailor X had been born in Nanzhou, in Pingdong County, Taiwan. He had served three years in the military in Mazu and had loved to paint ever since he was a child. This long-planned ship jumping was set up so that he could hew a place for himself in the new world, New York.

I first met X at a friend's house. He was small with a very dark complexion, and there was something strange about his eyes, his gaze direct and blank with a deeply hidden sadness. The woman who was with him was just the opposite: she was white-skinned and taller than him by almost a head. They stood against the wall, drinking and talking. Our host introduced X to me and said that he was a famous conceptual artist. The tall girl corrected him, saying, "He is a world-class master." When the liquor was gone and the guests had dispersed, the Master offered to drive me back to Manhattan. He drove a pickup truck with a topper. The woman was getting out after me, so she squeezed into the narrow back seat, arms and legs sticking out awkwardly.

X drove very steadily, with none of the bluster of a neophyte artist. I asked what school he belonged to and he answered casually. It turned out that he had been the very person who had made such a great ruckus in Chinese and American art circles twenty years earlier. As I was part of a painter's family, I had been as deeply impressed as everyone else at the time. He turned out to be quite introverted. I reflected that when a person is alone for a long time, other people become unimportant—mere projections on an imaginary wall.

After coming to New York, he got a job and considered what to do next with his art. Early works showed a tendency for self-mutilation, such as diving off a roof into a pit of feces, which ended up breaking both of his legs. Lamely feeling his way along, he clarified his ideas and created four year-long pieces in a row.

From 1978 to 1979, he imprisoned himself in a cage that was a ten-by-ten-meter square and two meters tall. For an entire year, he did not talk, read, listen to a radio, or watch TV. That was the year that my friends and I were devising ways to stay out of prison, but X did us one better, first locking himself up, and then worrying about it later. On the day he entered the cage, a lawyer pasted on a seal, and broke the same seal when he emerged a year later. Each day, friends delivered his meals. If he was not satisfied with the food, all he could do in protest was throw down his bowl. His bed was home and walking around the cell counted as going out. He made a mark on the wall for every day, a grand total of three hundred sixty-five marks. As he saw it, everyone has their own cage, but we are rarely aware of it.

Beginning in the spring of 1980, he locked himself in the same cage, dressed in a work uniform, and punched a time clock every hour for a year. To be more precise, he bought a Japanese time clock, and hooked it up to his watch and a speaker so that thirty seconds before every hour it would sound. This was just the opposite of his semi-hibernation of the first year—he became the world's busiest person and punched his card twenty-four times a day. He said that punching the card gradually became like a cripple's walk, becoming more and more natural. In his view, everything people do expends their limited lifespan, but what we call time is unlimited. By punching his card, he magnified the ridiculous relationship between time and human life.

The third piece was a year of living outdoors that began in the summer of 1981. He was not allowed to enter any buildings, subways, caves, tents, automobiles, trains, airplanes, boats, and the like. Carrying his sleeping bag on his back, he joined the ranks of the homeless on the streets of New York. He was better off than the homeless in that he had money and could keep his belly full, but unlike them, he could not dive into the subway, under a bridge, or into an abandoned building to sleep. That year the winter was exceptionally cold in New York, falling to thirty-eight degrees below zero on some nights. He wore all his clothes at once and stayed warm by fires. If he reclined, he would freeze to death. People are even crueler than nature. Once, while he was drinking tea near a factory, the manager chased him away, cursing and beating him. He defended himself with a cudgel he kept for protection. When the police arrived, he took out the newspaper article about himself, and managed to somehow fumble his way out of the situation. Not long after that, the same boss saw him on the street, and called the police again. This time they paid no attention to his artistic principles, and locked him up for fifteen hours. He spent some money to get a lawyer. On the day of his trial, the judge agreed to let him stay outdoors. Due to the lawyer's eloquent stubbornness and the judge's sympathy, he was finally released. Except for those fifteen hours, he lived outdoors for a year like a lone wolf, becoming a spectator to human civilization.

On July 4th, 1983, X and a female American artist named Linda tied themselves together at the waist with an eight-foot rope for one year. The two were not to touch. They washed and used the same toilet. They had to stay together to walk the dog, and when hosting and visiting their respective friends. It was more of a problem whenever they quarreled. Once, he wanted to take a bath, but Linda got angry and stormed out, almost dragging him into the street bare-assed. When they got along, they worked and made money, taught together, and flew to other cities to speak. By the time they finally split up in 1984, they couldn't stand each other.

From 1985 to 1986, he refused to make any art, or to talk about art for a year. Starting on December 31, 1986, until the last day of the twentieth century—a full 13 years—he made no public art. In my opinion, these last two announcements were superfluous: after the general retires, he no longer talks about war. During that time he married twice, and divorced twice. He told me that he was busy remodeling his house in Brooklyn as he wanted to invite artists from all over the world to live and work there for free.

12

EVERY WEDNESDAY AT NOON, I take the Number 9 subway to Penn Station where I first buy a copy of the *New York Times*, and then ride the 12:15 train to Long Island. On the train, I wrestle with the newspaper, the events concealed in another language making me sleepy, until the speakers crackle and I put on my bifocals and rush out the door, everything a haze. I then surge along with the crowd to a double-decker bus, climb to the second level, throw the newspaper aside, and gaze out the window at the scenery. After leaving New York, the air gets fresher. Trees, hills, streams, and white houses pass by in a flash. At 2:05 P.M., I arrive in Stony Brook.

Not long after moving to New York, I stumbled onto a job through a friend's introduction—teaching a poetry workshop in the English department of the State University of New York at Stony Brook. Because of transportation difficulties, the class met once a week, on Wednesdays. As for my English, even if the roles were switched and I were to be one of the students, I still would not be able to pass. But I thought to myself: In the U.S., the bold survive and the timid starve, and besides, poetry is ambiguous anyway, teaching it in a language that I don't speak fluently is even better. On the first day of class, I had a sort of pre-execution feeling, my scalp went numb and my entire body went cold.

The workshop ran from four until six, followed by three hours of individual conferences. I had to talk until I was completely out of words, utterly speechless, and so exhausted that my soul took flight. As soon as I saw the last student out and locked the door, I wrapped my overcoat tightly around myself and walked shivering through the clustered buildings and the parking lot, determined to make the 8:40 train to New York no matter what.

Most of my students were local and didn't have a New Yorker's shrewdness and hypersensitivity. I found it strange that in this place, only one hundred miles from New York, not only the face of the land, but even the people were different. Michael was ruddy-faced, his cheeks were covered with whiskers, his hair a tousled mess. He was sloppy, like an unfinished sketch for a portrait, and had a loud voice, sometimes calling me "professor," and sometimes "captain." At each break, he would shout, "Hot dog time!" and rush out the door. He told me that he had just broken up with his girlfriend, and now there were two candidates for the position. From the tone of his voice, you would have thought he worked in the White House, deciding which candidate was qualified to enter. He worked in a newsstand thirty hours a week and knew world affairs like the back of his hand, probably better than the president. He was a conservative Catholic, yet hoped for revolution, and was thus as confused as his poems.

Anna was an immaculate girl who blushed whenever she spoke and was always quiet in class. At first, her efforts were uneven, but later she wrote some amazing lines, making me, her teacher, rather pleased with myself. Christina was a fifty-year-old professional, the wife of a professor in the art department. She took this class simply because she loved poetry.

While she was without a doubt the most diligent student in the class, revising each poem numerous times, she didn't make great progress. She was immersed in fantasy. Poetry allowed her to soar away from the monotony of middle-class American life.

Winter passed into spring. The little path to the train station reappeared beneath the snow as it melted in the sun. I walked full of conviction into the wind, making calls all over the world on my cell phone.

13

ACTUALLY, NEW YORKERS ARE VERY lonely people—you can tell by their eyes. In general, with the exception of those with mental problems, no one looks directly at anybody, and in such a densely populated place, this can be a real inconvenience. On the subway, for example, in order not to meet anyone's gaze, you have to read the paper, close your eyes and rest, or simply let your gaze roam aimlessly in space, like a sleepwalker. This skill takes years of practice to master. Of course, should a couple of beautiful women appear, the men will wake up and their unclean gazes will shine like lights in the fog. They never stare directly like country mice, but stealthily track them out of the corner of their eyes, seemingly unmoved, or even a little disgusted, as if to say, "So what? Don't bother me."

The "unmarried aristocracy" in New York is especially large. The reason is simple: Being single is the best way to preserve one's loneliness—with no spouse, no children, there is no fuss. Other than when they get together with friends

or family, singles generally dine alone at home, calling the
local Chinese restaurant for take-out—one sweet-and-sour
pork with an order of hot-and-sour soup—or else they get by
with some dry cheese, or gnaw on day-old bread. Their gazes
roam over the four walls like a fly in danger of falling into
the corner web; sometimes they talk to themselves. It is no
surprise that a large number of New Yorkers are on anti-
depressants.

If two solitudes are added together, there are sure to be
new troubles. Once I was flying from New York to Paris. As
soon as I boarded the plane, I was aware of my awkward situation. I was seated between a husband and wife from New
York. The woman was on the aisle and the man by the window. I immediately offered to change seats, but they refused.
At first I supposed that there were some relationship problems, and I was to be used as a shield between them, but this
was not the case. On the contrary, they were an extremely
warm old couple, with "dear," "sweetheart," or "baby" coming
out every time they opened their mouths, to the point where
it began to make my skin crawl. They were generally very
solicitous of each other—the husband dug out his wife's
slippers and her novel; the wife hid away a free bottle of wine
for her husband to drink in Paris. More incomprehensible
to me was that this couple, even though I was lodged between
them, chatted freely about everything—from New York
weather to Paris hotels, from fights among their relatives to
investing in the stock market. I sucked in my breath and flat-
tened myself against the back of my seat to allow them some
space for their conversation. It wasn't a big deal to play the
third party, but infringing on their right to privacy seemed
wrong. Again, I suggested changing places, and was met
with a unanimous rejection. It was then that I understood

that they had chosen their seats in advance, requiring a witness for their solitude.

Solitude does not correspond to silence. It has its own sound, which in New York expands limitlessly. First there are the police cars, ambulances, and fire trucks, which, in order to attract sufficient attention, are constantly raising their voices to the heavens. Urban dogs, crazed from long confinement, are only rarely let out onto the streets. So when they pay their respects to other dogs, they do it with a howl let loose from the depths of their bellies. As for New Yorkers, when they want to express something, many of them are only comfortable doing so in an uncompromising manner, raising their voices. Mouth agape, invariably interrupted by police sirens, they're forced to swallow their words.

14

MISS W IS A CENTRAL FIGURE in the Chinese cultural scene. It was really just a case of being in the right place at the right time. Some people beat their brains out trying to attain such a position—throwing money around or printing name cards with eighteen titles, but to no avail. Cultural circles are both real and abstract. No real power structure exists in them, and therefore the usual forms of power are not recognized. There is no head, only a central figure.

In 1988, when I first moved to New York, I arrived just in time for a thriving Chinese cultural scene. There were people who sang Camille, who danced the Black Swan, who played the *pipa* behind their own backs, and who had the leading roles in plays. There were also wealthy Red Guards, and cultural business agents, as well as tongue-tied leaders of the overseas Chinese community, middle-aged and half-crazy amateur women writers, along with some indeterminate characters like me. Though everybody in the city, no matter who, might be strangers to each other, everyone knew Miss W. Her disposition was charming, she enjoyed lively crowds, she was in on everything and met visitors from all corners of the world. She ran a literary group, provided support for a poetry journal, organized readings, and took in wandering writers and artists, weaving in and out of their scraps of paper.

She had written poetry since she was young, and was gorgeous—the poets of Taiwan pursued her in droves. In the midst of this fracas, a visiting Taiwanese student wordlessly won and married her, leaving the others gaping.

Her muddleheadedness could be counted as one of the most important aspects of her excellence as it effectively dissolved petty rivalries and the inevitable anxieties of urban existence. As a foreign student in the United States, she muddled her way into the Diaoyu Islands Incident, and was put on the Kuomintang blacklist, exiled for twenty years. She then muddled her way into becoming the editor-in-chief of a North American Chinese language newspaper, where she gathered together rebellious spirits from all over the world. The newspaper's financial resources were eventually cut off and it ceased publication, giving her a rare two-day rest. Then she let me rope her into working like a dog for *Today*, China's first *samizdat* magazine, which I edited.

In important matters she was easily distracted, and in small matters, she was even more distracted. One time she went to the post office to send contact lenses to her son, who was attending school in another state, and also stuffed in a hamburger she had just bought. When she returned home, she suddenly realized what she had done and immediately called her son and told him that under no circumstances was he to eat the hamburger. Another time, she cheerfully went to San Francisco to see a friend, but when she got off the plane, there was no one to meet her and she could not reach anyone on the phone. Only after she asked a police officer for assistance did she realize she had gotten on the wrong plane and had flown to Los Angeles. Mornings are impossible for her, and when she does have to be in Manhattan in the morning, she is basically a somnambulist. If someone she knows greets her, she will loudly warn them, "I am not awake yet, and I can't tell who you are!"

Miss W has a very special smile that simultaneously expresses a feeling of powerlessness about the world, while revealing a certain tolerance, like a nurse watching over a critically ill patient. One's heart feels much more real when one is with her, even if no words are exchanged.

She and her husband bought an old loft in SoHo that tripled in value over just a few years, so they sold it and moved to upstate New York. I think the move from Manhattan was difficult. Each time she comes to the city, she has to keep a schedule pinched between her fingers in order to rush to catch the train back to the suburbs. In the past, because of her youth, she was not afraid of this kind of thing; if she were late, she would just make the trip later. Now, when people are just beginning to relax and enjoy themselves, she has to make her good-byes and depart. Chinese cultural circles in New York have since gone into a decline, due in no small part to the paucity of trains to the suburbs.

15

AFTER A YEAR AND A half in New York, I still had no news of Old A. I heard he was back in China on business, though people were always bringing up stories about him, stories that became part of the legends of New York. Old A had most definitely been a professional storyteller in a previous life. His gift for fabrication, story development, and lively description was unsurpassed. Had he lived in more peaceful times, his stories would have been merely stories—the storyteller would have kept sufficient distance from his stories, and performer and audience could share the quick pleasures of the narration. But he was cast into the world in an age of disorder that stirred his stories and his own experiences together, combining narrator and audience into one body, making him agitated and frantic in his telling, afraid of missing the smallest detail in his narration.

I got to know him in 1979 when I transferred to the magazine where he worked. In Tianjin, the year that he turned thirteen, he was labeled a counterrevolutionary and attempted suicide by leaping into the river. During the Cultural Revolution, he and his father were dispatched to Xinjiang together. Branded again as counterrevolutionaries, they wandered widely. While begging for food in Xi'an, he made the acquaintance of the daughter of the head of the local Public Security Bureau. According to him, every day she would pass him pieces of steaming *laobing* (a kind of pancake) from a window in the back of the official residence, until one day the *laobing* suddenly became a pair of burning chopsticks aimed at his face—they had been found out by her father.

Not long after I'd met him, Old A's tongue got him in trouble with someone who arranged to have him beaten so severely that he lost most of the sight in his left eye. In the early '80s he was a frequent guest in my house, and each time he came, his stories developed in new ways, freely flowing, rising, falling, and then, at crucial moments, he would give a loud laugh, wipe his mouth, and abruptly rise to his feet: "Now, for the next episode." At some point, we'd asked him to find a match for a girl whom we first had him meet. The girl found herself unable to resist his marvelous stories and she became his wife.

Old A had a kind of unflappability in any situation. On the first day of the lunar New Year, he was on the outs with his wife, and showed up at our place alone. We had just bought a roast chicken for the New Year's celebration and served it on a platter to our guests. He told us all his sorrows, so full of pain, while at the same time gnawing, with skill and avidity, the roast chicken. As we stared, the chicken disappeared and at the end of his tale of misery, nothing remained but a pile of chicken bones.

The events of 1989 were an unfortunate confirmation of his predictions. He fled, and his stories reached new heights as he added new sections where the nine immortals crossed the ocean, and the beauty rescued the hero. First he went to Paris and then to New York, followed by marriage and then children. But living in New York was expensive and he had to find a way to earn a living. While strolling in Chinatown he noticed someone who had opened up shop as a fortune-teller. He went in to see if he could learn something, but the fortune-teller was very mediocre. He had always been interested in divination, so how difficult could it be to read a few more books on the subject? When Chinese people become suddenly wealthy and buy property, they never feel totally secure until they have someone check out the *fengshui* of the new property. Master A had all sorts of divinatory lore at his fingertips, and he dispensed pearls of precious advice. When word got out about him, there was no going back. First he set up appointments—and they were hard to squeeze in—then he was picked up and driven home, wined and dined by clients, and at the end of all this, he was given a red envelope stuffed with money.

When I saw him in New York later that year, he had grown sideways, his face had a well-fed sheen, and the half-blind left eye bulged out. But within this state of superficial excitement, I noticed that there was actually a kind of disquiet—to his customers, he was just another storyteller. Though he was making money, there was no further sense of participation, nor did his stories reach any new heights. In other words, New York could get along without him.

But this page in his life turned very quickly. One day I read an article analyzing the situation in the Taiwan Straits. The byline was by A, political analyst. Soon afterward, I saw him again on the Chinese language channel, earnestly speaking at a conference on cross-straits military issues. Once, he told me that Beijing and the Pentagon had each secretly contacted him and he hinted that whether World War III would be fought or not was up to him.

From *fengshui* master to military expert—there really is no meaningful dividing line. In fact, it even seems to be a logical development: from ancient to modern, rites before arms, from the array of the eight trigrams to missile blockades, peace is the most precious. Bored with telling stories, he moved directly into the business of history—cultivating himself, regulating his household, putting his family in order, running local government, and finally bringing peace to all under heaven.

16

New York has an underground world that corresponds proportionally to the height of its buildings, like a giant to his shadow and the dark night to the bright day. I recall the name of a popular song, "Daylight doesn't understand the darkness of night." I used to be skeptical, but after careful thought, I see that this really makes sense. If New York were to be psychoanalyzed, this underground world would no doubt be crucial.

Compared to the unbearable confusion on the surface, the subway represents order and is New York's resilient nervous system. By going down just once, you understand that this is the reason why the international metropolis does not go mad. In Manhattan, the subway really only has two directions: uptown and downtown. In principle, even an idiot can use it without getting too lost. If one gets confused aboveground, everything can be clarified underground. Most Americans have a unidirectional style of thinking—their goals are very clear, black and white are well-defined. Sometimes I want to explain to Americans just what kind of a place China is, but it's too difficult for me. The harder I try to explain, the more confused people look, and they invariably end up asking some absurd question, which leaves me frustrated and speechless—a dead end. "Daylight doesn't understand the darkness of night."

New York's first real subway was built in 1870, designed by the inventor Alfred E. Beach. He had the fantastic notion to use wind power—great fans blowing into enclosed tubes. A model was first shown at an exhibition, producing a great deal of commotion. But making the model into a viable means of transportation was far more difficult. Technical problems aside, the greater problem was the human aspect, namely the bosses who ran the world of New York politics. Without a nod from them, nothing could even begin. Beach then decided to proceed in an underground fashion. He rented the basement of a clothing store, where he had laborers work at night, carting away the earth they had dug up before the sun rose. In the greatest secrecy, over the course of only fifty nights, a 312-foot wind tunnel subway was finished, complete with a 120-foot-long luxury waiting room with oil paintings, a piano, and a fountain to relieve the anxieties of the claustrophobic. On February 26, 1870, Beach held a grand opening ceremony that astounded New York. Afterward, he made his plans public: After the passing of a public transportation bill that would give him building rights, he would privately raise five million dollars of capital and construct a line nearly five miles long, which would carry two hundred thousand passengers every day. The New York state legislature passed the bill. The bosses of the political machine were scared; this was a direct threat to the percentage they received on earnings of each omnibus. The puppet governor came up with a way to veto the transportation bill and a lawsuit dragged out in the courts for more than two years, ending with Beach's defeat, forcing him to seal up his subway. More than forty years later, in 1912, workers on the subway near City Hall accidentally knocked a hole in the wall of a silent subway waiting room.

17

M's FAMILY WAS ORIGINALLY FROM Hubei, but she was born and raised in Hong Kong, studied in Paris, and tested into the

United Nations as an interpreter. There she has worked, first in Geneva and then in New York, for the past twenty years. She is fluent in six or seven languages and can do simultaneous interpretation in three of them. She cooks Italian food, drinks French wine, reads English newspapers, and can speak to just about anyone she meets in their own language. Sometimes I wonder how large a part of her brain Chinese occupies. One's cultural allegiance is often in the unconscious. For example, the language in which one counts and curses, or the language one speaks in dreams. And in the final analysis, those whose spiritual bloodlines cannot be clearly delineated can all be counted as "cultural orphans." New York is supposed to be half foreigners, with their children occupying another fourth of the city—a veritable orphanage. As a result, "patriotism" is a term that doesn't exist in the New York lexicon.

New York is the site of encounters between people of all races, backgrounds, and experiences. Ten years ago, a friend brought me to M's apartment for dinner. She lived on the east side of Midtown Manhattan in a glass cage of twenty-seven stories. A parrot, Luke, looked down on the guests and sized us up from his perch. He continually repeated in English, "Luke wants peanuts." It was an evening filled with dirty jokes accenting the splendid food, fine wine, and piano music. Almost all of the men smoked, and the hostess opened a window, allowing the wind to carry the wisps away.

I have only known M since she's been a mother. Divorced for many years, she raised two boys on her own. In a city like New York, young people can be as fierce as tigers—and she had two of them. Just thinking about this made me worry on her behalf. Now, many years later, her two children have left home and are off at universities. Once, I took her to the movies, and we chose a film without knowing that it would deal with issues of youth drug use and violence. Less than five minutes into it, she couldn't take it any more and could not be persuaded to stay. All the way back, she hugged her shoulders, as if afraid of the cold.

I am the same age as M. Our experiences are entirely different, but we have one thing in common—we were both born under the sign of the migratory bird and thus share a passion for travel. For a few years she went mad, flying all over the world the minute she had any free time. At the U.N., she already had numerous opportunities to travel for business, but it was never enough for her; she devotedly paid travel agencies out of her own pocket. New York became a stopover, and her home a hotel that she was ready to leave at a moment's notice. She would even take an evening flight to Paris on Friday, spend two days touring around, stay out all night, and wind up half dead from exhaustion. But she always made it back to work on Monday.

M had always planned to retire early and move to Florence. But who would have thought that, after being a daughter-in-law for so many years, she would finally find her way into the position of mother-in-law by receiving a promotion and becoming the head of the U.N. Interpretation Center with hundreds of language geniuses under her charge. After all, what we want and what we get are seldom the same thing. I recall her parrot's words: "Luke wants peanuts. . . ."

18

THE PLANE ARRIVED punctually at Newark Airport. Today is Tuesday, the third week after 9/11. During my flight, several armed National Guardsmen sullenly looked the passengers over. Pulling my luggage, I went to the bus counter to buy a ticket. The people waiting for the bus were wrapped in silence, each with their own imponderables. The bus finally arrived, and with much coughing and panting, made its rounds of the airport, scooping up the odd passenger. Save for the driver's half-grimace visible in the rearview mirror, I could only see the backs of the other passengers' heads. Manhattan appeared. The sun was setting, the city's eyeteeth, the twin towers of the World Trade Center had been pulled, and thick smoke billowed out of the pit up to the heavens. I stepped off the bus at Forty-second Street, got lost, and finally hailed a cab that rushed me to the East Village.

At first, New Yorkers seemed no different than before, going about their business as usual. But on closer inspection, it became clear that a shadow obscured their faces. Only toward evening would they relax, perhaps because the shadows of night were thicker, letting people release a sigh of relief. We walked. The weather was hot and stuffy, and the air was filled with a strong burning smell. Here and there on street corners and beside light posts were small altars in disarray—candle flames flickered in the wind next to the photos of the missing.

I lived in New York for a total of six months, and by the time I left, I had grown rather fond of the city. This same city that saps one's energy, where the young thrive because energy is what they have and what they need to release—leaping, colliding, squeezing, sweating, and bleeding within the smallest of spaces. The same city the older generations love because of nostalgia. When the expenditure of energy is great, there will certainly be great changes, things are renewed quickly, but they also grow old even more quickly. Indeed, New York is a truly nostalgic destination. It's like driving a car: Look

straight ahead, don't look back, just let your mind idle, perfectly aware of everything that has disappeared behind you.

Last spring I participated in a reading in New York with a
black woman poet. Her poem about New York pigeons left a
deep impression on me. Just about every city has pigeons, but
the pigeons and the fate of the pigeons are completely different in different cities. For example, the pigeons in Paris live
much more comfortably. The old buildings are elegant and
open, and from the bread crumbs offered by tourists to the
garbage of restaurants, they have everything they could possibly need. When I was in Sarajevo, the pigeons lived lives filled
with shock—if it wasn't shells, it was bullets, explosions and
shootings rarely stopping for even a couple of days. The
pigeons were also forced to endure hunger, and each of them
needed to see a therapist.

The situation of pigeons in New York is entirely different.
First of all, the geography is dangerous. In abysses hundreds
of meters deep, they must learn from birth to take off and
land vertically, without a safety net. Then there are the innumerable traps of glass, which they must learn to recognize
and avoid, otherwise one moment's inattention could lead to
a fatal collision. Add to this the exhaust, noise, and the blind-
ness of car tires. Though there is no lack of food and drink,
their environment makes them narrow and cold and full of
aggression. Pigeons are actually rather fierce and cruel birds,
fond of strife, the weak among them falling prey to the strong
as they form their own systems of power—quite similar to
human systems. Aside from the interrelationship of the food
chain, their lives do not intersect with those of human beings.
They are spectators. When you and a pigeon stare at each
other through a window, the pigeon is curious, and in the

rapid focus of its eyes it seizes your awkward expression, but it is not at all interested in entering your life.

One morning, two great metal birds crashed into Manhattan's two tallest buildings, bringing about a great conflagration. The huge noise and the wave of heat startled the pigeons roosting there, and with a flutter of wings they flew off, wheeling into the sky.

LUNCH

I

AT 12:30 P.M., I ring the doorbell of New Directions Publishing on the nineteenth floor of 80 Eighth Avenue in Manhattan, and Peggy comes out to greet me. Whenever I am in New York, she and Griselda take me out for lunch. Along with Eliot, who lives nearby, our foursome dines on a green, for-company-use-only American Express card. But I wanted to do things differently this time and skip lunch, so when I arrived in New York—without calling ahead—I dove alone into the sea of humanity. But to my surprise, while the crowds dispersed after a memorial reading for Octavio Paz at the Metropolitan Museum of Art, Peggy materialized in front of me and, brooking no excuses, fixed a lunch date.

Peggy Fox is my editor as well as the Managing Director and Vice President of New Directions.* From the back windows of her house on the upper Hudson, you can see the river through the thick reeds. Eliot and I visited her home in the spring of 1992. After a meal cooked by her husband, we walked

---

* This essay was written in 1999, four years before Griselda Ohannessian retired and Peggy Fox became President and Publisher. Griselda remains a Director and Trustee.

along a mile-long pier that stretches out into the Hudson. A monument at the end of the pier marks the spot where, during the Second World War, many American boys said farewell to their loved ones, never to return. James Laughlin passed away two years ago, and unfortunately I never had the opportunity to meet him. The publishing house has since become a matriarchy where most of the senior editors are women—mother hens who have hatched and reared some of our generation's most masculine literature.

Eliot arrives late. As Paz's English translator, he has been run almost to death over the past couple of days. Grand memorial activities in honor of Paz have been held in New York and Washington, culminating in the reading at the Met, where Eliot was placed, according to alphabetical order, at the very end. Sitting beside me, he was anxious but able to control himself. Still, a match brushed against his body would probably have ignited. The American Poet Laureate, Robert Pinsky, acted as master of ceremonies and in tying the various readings together used Eliot as the closing knot, speaking highly of him. Before reading the final section of Paz's *Sunstone*, Eliot, his voice choked with emotion, begins, "Thirty years ago, only a few blocks from here, Paz and I gave our first reading together. It is strange now to have the translations without the original."

Griselda finally shows up. She is over seventy and has just recovered from pneumonia. She is not yet very steady on her feet, but remains the head of the publishing house and in charge of the American Express card, though illness and age are slowly forcing her into retirement. Her father, Schulyer Jackson, was a poet and literary critic. Some sixty years ago, the English poet Robert Graves and his companion, Laura Riding, spent a summer with Griselda's family. Her father and Laura fell madly in love, and their relationship drove her mother into a breakdown. Her father and Laura moved to Florida, living in seclusion on a grapefruit farm until their deaths. In those forty years, they collaborated on an English dictionary in which each word had one and only one meaning. It was neither completed nor published. Griselda only rarely saw her father after that summer.

The four of us go down to ground level from the nineteenth floor, cross the street, turn a corner and make straight for Café de Bruxelles. We have tried several other places over the past ten years but have never been very pleased with any of them. Experimentation is just experimentation, but it is the way that traditions get started.

Bruxelles is decorated mostly in dark greens, very old school in a kind of prewar European flavor. The atmosphere is relaxed but decorous, there are no young people or alcoholics, and I would guess that most of the people around us are regulars. The four tables by the windows turn under the ever-changing light from outside. Most of the time we take the same corner table, perhaps for a certain feeling of stability. On overcast or rainy days, the four tables at last become still. Summer sunlight, filtered by the window, is no longer so violently bright. When winter comes, dappled and shifting light is like an illusion.

The waiters, polite without exaggeration, are always ready to disappear.

2

THERE ARE SOME THINGS IN New York that never change. For the past ten years we, these same four people have gone to the same restaurant, sat at the same table, and talked over the same subjects. Even our tastes have gradually become more and more similar. Today, though, Griselda orders calf's liver; Peggy, Eliot, and I all opt for the duck salad. And to drink? All four of us have iced tea. As is our custom, we also ask for two orders of pommes frites with mayonnaise.

First we talk about the resounding success of the Paz reading. Since the hall had filled up quickly more than a thousand people had to be turned away, including some sponsors of the reading and Mexican senators. Peggy says she was stopped at the gate, but fortunately a party of Mexican politicians arrived at the same time. She announced that she was Paz's publisher, and thus literature slipped into the hall via politics.

I say that it was Paz, his individual charm, that brought together two groups that under normal circumstances did not interact: the diverse elements of the American poetry scene and the politicians and diplomats. The reading was like a reunion of a family deep in reconciliation, the only out-siders being a Swedish poet and I. "You were but a babe among them," Griselda interjects. She tells me that the rather lanky fellow with the gray hair had been Kennedy's special ad-visor. "It is simply amazing! Almost half a century has gone by and he is still alive!" Griselda sighs. Everyone stares at the table, as if we had seen a ghost. "Nobody has ever understood Paz's politics," Eliot says, devouring a French fry. "Actually, it is very simple. By American standards, he was a leftist, but by Latin American standards he is considered a rightist since he was an anti-communist and anti-Castro . . . and lots of Latin American writers support Castro."

The duck salads arrive. The kitchen is like a drama's un-spoken lines, hiding behind literature and politics and then taking them by surprise. Our stomachs are suddenly awake, throbbing like hearts. For a long time the only thing that can be heard is the clanking of forks and knives. Everyone has stopped speaking, concentrating instead on the flavor of the duck, the texture of the salad greens, and the color and sheen of the dressing. The sounds of cars and footsteps leak in and a human shadow slides across the window. The sunlight dazzles. Sunlight is, in fact, New York City's real master. Yesterday morning, a French photojournalist taking my picture led me out in the middle of the street in pursuit of sunlight. I see New York's light through a photographer's eyes: groping its way through groves of buildings, refracting, and then in an instant, gone.

I ask Eliot about the crime rate in New York. On the morning of my second day back, I was at a coffee shop at the corner of Lexington Avenue and Thirty-first Street drinking coffee and reading a Chinese newspaper. There was an item about Yo-Yo Ma losing, then regaining, his cello. Getting out of a cab, he had forgotten to take his two and a half million-dollar cello out of the trunk. After he reported the loss, the entire New York police force was mobilized to find the taxi. Four hours later the cello was back in Yo-Yo Ma's hands; his performance that evening wasn't even delayed. As I was reading that very article, a thief nimbly slipped away with my book bag. It was over before you could say "knife." When it dawned on me what had happened, I took a look around, sizing everyone up—but they all appeared to be upright, law-abiding citizens. Peggy and Griselda immediately hug their bags closer to themselves, as though afraid they will sprout wings and fly away. Eliot rolls his eyes, shakes his head and says, with a note of reproof in his voice, "This is New York." Eliot has no choice but to reprove those of us from the countryside whenever we draw attention to the failings of city dwellers.

I ask Eliot what he thinks of Mayor Giuliani. "He's a total fascist!" Eliot explodes. "Even for a barbecue in the park, you need authorization if it's more than twenty people. That's a violation of the right to free assembly! And don't even mention the Brooklyn incident!"

After the dishes are cleared away, the four of us have coffee. The conversation turns to next year's election. Eliot sighs and says he doesn't know who to vote for. He explains to me that Kansas has recently passed a bill that denies the theory of evolution and makes Judeo-Christian creationism the basic classroom curriculum.

"If the world has only existed for ten thousand years, then how do you explain fossils?" Eliot shrugs and continues by explaining Borges's essay about God creating the earth with fossils. "Yet in order to win votes there, Gore took no stand on the issue." Peggy and Griselda nod. Even these American leftists are fed up with the Democratic Party. Political prospects look as dark as the coffee.

I ask Peggy why there is no third political power in American politics. "A Reform Party has sprung up, but it is unlikely that it will become a real third power." Peggy patiently explains the American electoral process to me.

"Why have almost all current American presidential candidates been lawyers?" I ask. This is the outsider's privilege—to ask questions without shame or inhibition. Peggy and Griselda one by one tick off a few recent presidential candidates on their fingers before conceding that, sure enough, I am right.

"Don't the thinking and rhetoric of the legal trade influence American politics?" I ask.

"They use legal jargon to accomplish their ends through calculation and misdirection," Peggy says.

Lunch is over and we say good-bye at the door. The sunlight is bright and alluring; this is the last golden moment of fall. For some reason, I think of Manet's *Le Déjeuner sur l'herbe*, when in reality this painting has nothing to do with our lunch at Bruxelles.

PARIS STORIES

THE FIRST TIME I MET Y was in the spring of 1991, when I was giving a reading at the Pompidou Center. After the reading, Y came over with his girlfriend to get his book autographed. I turned and, taking him for one of the photographers, left the hall, pulling him with me down to the restaurant. Fortunately, he dealt calmly with this unexpected development, making the most of my mistake.

On June 4, 1989, he was in China working as a photo editor for a publishing house. Miraculously, he got unofficial access to the execution grounds through his connections, arriving just as they were shooting one of the "violent elements" that they had grabbed at random off the street. From three paces away, he photographed the gruesome scene. Returning home, he watched six movies in a row, but nothing helped. The cry of the young man before his execution still rang in his ears: "Twenty years from now, I will be reborn a hero!"

In 1990, Y accepted an invitation to Paris. As soon as his feet hit the ground, he published those photos in the French pictorials *Match* and *Time*, and won an international photography award. After that, he was blacklisted, his house was searched, and he promptly joined the ranks of the exiled.

Other exiles were in trouble with China, but Y was in trouble with the Public Security Bureau. Even if the others could return one day, he would have to keep going forward alone.

When Y was younger he did field survey work, scrambling though the mountainous wilds of southwest China for eight years. For him, Paris was much too narrow, too cultured. He drove a dirty BMW up and down the Parisian streets. Once he settled down there, he didn't take part in the overseas democracy movement but instead joined the wider class of working people as a photographer of purses. People from Wenzhou had become famous for the purses they made and almost monopolized the French handbag market. The value of each handbag depended entirely on advertising, which was a perfect fit with his own expertise. Handbags delivered up from dark basement workshops had to pass through his hands before being slung over the shoulders of beautiful women. "*Click*, 200 francs. *Click*, 200 francs," was his contented description of his production procedure.

2

I LIVED AT NUMBER 7 rue de Venise. Rue de Venise, which is only a bit more than two meters wide and one hundred meters long is possibly the shortest alley in Paris. Though my street was right next to the Pompidou Center, few tourists ever found their way down this fold within Beaubourg Plaza. Those of us who lived here enjoyed a flea's concealed vantage point. For example, looking out at the Pompidou Center's newly constructed mammoth television screen from the depths of our alley was like a peasant's peek at modernization. There were a number of bars in the neighborhood. Drunks would appear and disappear in the middle of the night, screaming and carrying on, often waking us from our dreams.

Whenever I went to the Troisième Arrondissement to pick up some food on Wenzhou Street, I had to pass through the plaza. Sunlight glittered off the glass and metal pipes of the museum; tourists were swallowed into a giant, mechanical stomach and then spat back out as if they were indigestible refuse. In my view, the Pompidou Center was built by French politicians as a memorial to themselves, a kind of promise to the future. This promise also has a kind of playful quality and cannot be taken too seriously. And it is precisely this playfulness that is an important element of French culture, visible in everything from their movies, fashion, and performing arts to their philosophical thought.

Paris was the first foreign city I got to know well. I was introduced to the city by Russian writer Ehrenburg's memoir, *People, Years, Life*. Because he had taken part in underground work before the October Revolution, he fled to Paris, where he stayed for ten years. During that time, the city was home to people from all walks of life—artists, writers, exiles, dreamers, and impoverished aristocrats from every country. This four-volume set with its yellowed pages was almost a Bible to the underground Chinese poets of the seventies. What we read when we are young often makes little sense, but influences us for the rest of our lives. I read *People, Years, Life* countless times, which gave rise to a strange nostalgia for a city I had never been to.

In July, 1985, I came to Paris for the first time. It was a dizzying summer. Following Ehrenburg's "map," I walked the streets, great and small, of the city. The old Paris was still there, but it had a different face. I found few traces of that tumultuous life described in his book. In Montmartre, I accidentally wandered into a group of Japanese tourists. When I finally made it to a coffee shop and was able to sit down, I paid for a cola with a two-hundred-franc note I had borrowed from a friend; the waiter, with a devious smile, brought me back only forty.

3

Y DROVE ME OUT TO see Sir X. Sir X had bought a house on the outskirts of Paris and led a life of semi-eremitic solitude. We first stopped in Chinatown to buy some cakes and got stuck in a traffic jam. It took us forever to get out of the city. Trapped in the complex maneuvers of several large trucks, we finally got in touch with Sir X on his cell and, with much difficulty, found the small town where he lived.

Sir X came out to welcome us. His hair was graying and he walked with a slight hunch, as though bowing in respect before the deepening twilight. These days there aren't many left like him. Honest and kind, he has a great breadth of experience, a bellyful of knowledge, and is also a great conversationalist. He should have led a professor's peaceful life, but as it turned out, he was swept up in the Tiananmen events, and became a wanted man throughout China. He was a fugitive for a long time, and finally escaped through the underground on a fishing boat. But not long after the boat set out to sea, they were chased down by a patrol cruiser and towed into the harbor to be searched. With no other choice, the ship's captain made him jump overboard and swim for land. Fortunately, he had grown up around the Yangzi River and was a good swimmer as he had to swim for hours, passing through an oyster bed where he was almost cut to ribbons. But the gods smiled on him for when he reached the shore the Liberation Army soldiers were having lunch and had not posted any sentries. After dressing his wounds, he fled again, first to Hong Kong and then to Paris.

Sir X once spent six years translating Sartre's *Being and Nothingness*. Then, years later, under the mysterious guidance of Sartre's spirit, he settled in Paris. It is as if he has been traveling on a long road for the sake of a philosophical question, one for which he uses his life as proof: his exile is both a void and a forced choice, like the rendezvous between being and nothingness.

After I came to Paris to speak in 1991, I got together with a few friends. It was then that I met Sir X, who spoke little but was congenial. The next day, he invited me to his house for a few drinks. Sir X had a very endearing quality. Unperturbed by adversity, he could take up and then set aside the weightiest of matters, dissolving them by making fun of himself. There are not many Chinese intellectuals who know how to laugh at themselves, and thus they always miss the mark when they try, overdoing it or not doing it enough. Sir X worked silently in exile, writing for himself, filtering his reflections from his years abroad onto paper.

His wife, a former student of his, was much younger. They had two daughters in quick succession, so that along with his wife's younger brother and his wife, it was a full house. Sir X was a formidable cook. With just a whip of his apron and some clanking around the kitchen, there would be a table spread with delicious food; and when the strong spirits were poured, a flush of pleasurable anticipation rose in our hearts.

It is easy to imagine with what style he must have taught his classes in Beijing. But these days, though far from a cultural center and busy making a living, he seldom had such loyal listeners. Smacking his lips as he drank liquor, he could rattle on about any topic—ancient, modern, Chinese, or foreign. After his cup was filled three times, he would come at last to the topic of living overseas, and his mood would inevitably darken.

When we said farewell, the night was as cool as water.

4

"I LOVE YOU, CAPITAL OF ten thousand evils." Baudelaire was the first modern poet to write specifically about Paris, and his poems are a malediction against the city. During the course of his life in Paris, he moved forty-two times, from 13 rue Hautefeuille in the Latin Quarter all the way to the cemetery at Montparnasse. I love to move, but not to the nearly crazed extent of Baudelaire.

Perhaps his restlessness was due to the quality of light in the city in which he was born and raised. Paris has a unique sort of light due to the protean weather, reflections off the river, the winding of the streets, and the effects of lamplight. I would guess that Baudelaire was a congenital insomniac. As there were no extra-strength sleeping pills, he was doomed to wander the streets at night. The gaslights added weight to the spectral feeling in his poetry. The growing gap between the rich and the poor and the rapid urban expansion of the Second Empire were hard for the poet to adapt to. Pounding a table, he rose to his feet and joined the Revolution of 1848.

In the summer of 1995, my parents and daughter visited me in Paris. I rented a place for them in the Septième Arrondissement, a place where time seemed to run in reverse. Early in the morning, it was the bejeweled old ladies who walked the street. With a self-assured sway to their gait and their eyes rolled upward, they greeted each other in the drawling tones of the elite. I was staying with a friend in a neighborhood filled with the standardized ranks of third world buildings. Children of every color played noisily together with boundless energy, their French clipped and unpleasant to the ear. At any moment, they were ready to take over the management of the city.

When I came to Paris from New York, Y picked me up at Charles de Gaulle Airport. He spread open a newspaper: the day before had been the Paris mayoral election; the left had won. They said that it was the first time since the Paris Commune in 1871 that the left had control of the city government.

5

As soon as I got to Paris, I called N. She was not home, so I left a message. She called me back later that evening. "So, you've finally arrived," she said with a laugh.

N had lived in an attic in a wealthy neighborhood for many years. Cramped and dark, with no shower, it was a room that servants used to live in. She was born and raised in Guangxi, studied and taught in Hong Kong, and then moved to Paris in 1989 to earn her doctorate. She traveled the world in pursuit of love. Her boyfriend was French, married, had a family, and could not get a divorce. I brought her a copy of Ha Jin's novel *Waiting*.

"It's a good title. When you think about it, everything is a process. Sometimes I think the goal isn't that important," she told me with a sigh.

N invited me to her place for lunch. After she got her degree, she worked for a while in the Museum of the Middle Ages, then finally found a teaching position at a university. Now in somewhat easier circumstances, she had moved to a fashionable section of the Latin Quarter, close to a café that Sartre used to frequent. Her place was small and cozy; pictures occupied most of the space. There was no kitchen, and the stove was behind a small counter. She served food like a waitress in a bar.

It was a wet, early spring day; a damp breeze blew in through the open window. There's a kind of old-fashioned warmth in the Chinese cultural circle in Paris, something seldom encountered in other places.

Z arrived late. This Tiananmen square protestor had just received a French doctorate in sociology, and since he had not been able to find work, he was staying at home and taking care of his children. He used to be a rash young fellow, but now he looked pale and underfed. Without a doubt, he had the most potential of anyone in the "Tiananmen generation." By coincidence, Z's savior, H, was also there. He had a full beard and could sing sorrowful and salty tunes from Shanbei. After the Tiananmen crackdown, Z and another protester fled and took shelter with him. Endangering life and limb for his friends, H left his family behind.

When the bottle ran dry and the guests had departed, N and I walked to a nearby bookstore. Paris bookstores are simple and modest, a far cry from the crass displays and marketing methods of American bookstores. Customers enjoy a relaxed and intimate connection with the books.

Coming out of the bookstore, a rainstorm greeted us and we took shelter in a coffee shop near the Académie Française, a café that writers and publishers frequent. It was dusk and the lamps flickered on. N spoke about China's death penalty, about an instinctive feeling women have to procreate, and then about her research projects and her life. I faced the window, looking at the people panicking in the rain. Brightly colored umbrellas, one after another, opened like broken flowers.

6

I WANDERED AIMLESSLY ALONG THE SEINE. The booksellers' stalls, lined up in a row along the river, were all closed, the wooden crates locked shut, most likely awaiting the weekend or the summer before opening again. I wondered how this ancient trade managed to continue; in any other country it would have disappeared long ago without a trace. Perhaps it has something to do with the nostalgia of the French and their pursuit of leisure, which is a necessary condition for creativity. These days such leisure is disappearing due to the pursuit of so-called material comforts. But leisure is at the very root of comfort. In the dark night of modernization, many people have forgotten leisure can be a true source of light.

I turned into a small square by the Louvre. It was still early and there were few tourists. I.M. Pei's glass pyramid flashed with a dim blue light. This palace was born at the end

of the eleventh century as a fort built at the order of King
Philippe Auguste during the Crusades. Later, each king will-
fully rebuilt the palace in accordance with his own tastes,
completely altering its original appearance and stripping it of
any character. I'm actually not very fond of this palace. It feels
oppressive. While it is on one hand the pride of the French,
it also more or less reflects their weaknesses—vanity and
pomposity.

I ordered a spring roll, some fish and noodles, and a
Tsingtao beer at a small restaurant on Wenzhou Street. While
reading a Chinese newspaper, I ate. After my meal, I returned
to my apartment for a nap. I was soon awakened by someone
in the street shouting my name. I groggily shouted back a
reply, and our voices rose and fell in turn, like two yodelers in
the Alps. Then someone pounded on my door. It was Y. I had
disconnected the phone before my nap and the door inter-
com was broken.

Y always carried a bulging plastic bag. I asked him
whether it had reached the point where he hated taking pictures of handbags. "Not at all. It's my rice bowl," he replied,
gesturing with his hands, ashes from his cigarette scattering
over the table.

Photographing handbags was a periodic activity. When Y
was busy with his work, he continued without stopping for
months at a time. Once the work was finished, he had as
much free time as a goldfish. Rising at noon, he would first
buy a Chinese newspaper then go to a coffee shop where he
read it front to back. Then he would spend the entire day
playing *weiqi* (go) at a Sichuan restaurant not far from where I
lived. I think he generally favored the black pieces—night
locked in battle with day. But despite so much practice, he
made absolutely no progress in his technique. Even now,

when his opponent has a four-piece handicap, it isn't certain he will win.

A friend once called Y from Germany and commented on his life in exile: "What the hell do you think you're doing?! Playing a joke on history? Think about it. One dynasty lasts hundreds of years, but how long does one person live? At the most, several decades. How many lifetimes do you think you can suffer like this?" Y laughed to himself but did not answer. He wants to trick history; it is his fate. The way he passes his time is certainly tied to this fact, and the reason is simple—he arrived here from death.

7

C IS MY FRENCH TRANSLATOR. She teaches Chinese literature in Paris. She has been divorced for many years and has raised two children on her own. She is French, but married a Chinese man many years ago and so has a Chinese surname that she kept after her divorce—a final connection to China.

We went out for lunch. The sun jerked like a flashlight and then disappeared; the sky clouded over. After the long winter had finally passed, spring in Paris was a joke. The meticulous wool coat C wore was a bargain find at an outdoor market. According to her, it was made by a famous tailor, her eyes sparkling when she told me this. C has none of the vanity of French women professionals. The majority of the furniture at her house was picked up off the street and doesn't match, but it all goes together, like a family of orphans.

There is a kind of tragedy in C's character, but this tragedy is concealed by the mundane details of day-to-day life.

She is also a perfectionist. I never met her Chinese husband. Their love was tied up with the revolutionary fire of '68. Tired of the violence, they took a bus to Spain. Whenever she tells this story, a deep blush spreads over her face.

I used to stay at her place whenever I was in Paris. Her house was in a small town at the outskirts of the city on a quiet street named Espérance, a flower bed and a big willow tree in her yard. The house was very small when she bought it, but because of the space her children needed, the house was endlessly expanded, most of the work done with her own two hands. When she ran out of money, C had no choice but to stop work and wait until she could afford more building materials. When her daughters grew up and moved away, the house, still unfinished, became empty in an instant.

Her street did not have much hope to give. Two years ago, a gale uprooted the willow; then, after successive years of drought, the foundation shifted, and great cracks appeared in the house. She had insurance, but the construction of the reinforcements dragged on and on. And what was even more unfortunate was that she loved to dance ballet, but her legs refused to cooperate. After she had an operation on the semilunar valve in her left knee, and had to hop around like a wounded bird for many months, her right leg started acting up with the same problem.

These days, she sits in her unsteady tower translating and preparing for classes. She has always been a high-strung person, and the world seems set on making things difficult for her. But she has her own way of dealing with things; besides dancing, she writes poetry and takes photographs. And at least in an aesthetic sense, she expresses her objection to her fate.

8

ONE SUMMER MORNING TWO years ago, a friend of mine who lived in Paris took me for a walk. On the bridge leading to Notre Dame de Paris, he impulsively called O, who lived nearby. Luckily, O was home so we dropped by. She was almost seventy, a second-generation Russian immigrant, and a solitary widow. She had learned Chinese and used to be the editor-in-chief for the *UNESCO Courier*. We had once celebrated Chinese New Year together at a friend's house. She was opposed to setting out one's views in writing and felt that writing in itself was always colored to some degree by the desire for material gain, while the most magnificent things in the world cannot be captured by the written word, like the reflections of Christ or Confucius.

O's house was right on the Seine, sunlight reflecting off the river moved restlessly on the windowpanes. She was wearing a nightgown and her graying hair hung loosely past her shoulders. She said that she was sick, and ushered us into the bedroom where she took out two long-stemmed glasses and filled them with pink champagne. Her house was like a miniature anthropological museum. A skull was set on the bedside table, and the coffee table was a lid of a coffin from an ancient Burmese tomb.

She waited until we were seated and told us about an incident that had taken place over the previous weekend, her gestures infused with excitement. Not long ago, she had received an invitation to see a performance of Gorky's play *The Lower Depths*, which was being staged by some Russian immigrants. Bringing along two bottles of champagne, she made her way with some difficulty to an abandoned cellar on a small street.

"It was called rue de Paradis," she said with a strange smile. "How ironic."

The Russians who lived in the cellar were dressed in rags and their eyes did not leave the two bottles of champagne in her hands. She soon realized she was the only one invited to the performance. There was no stage and no lights; almost all the residents played a role. They came and went, their lines poured out naturally—this was no play, it was life itself.

After the performance was over, she remained and ate a meal with them, just bread and salt. The fine champagne she brought with her was finished the instant the bottles were opened. Their eyes moved around in the darkness. "It has been a long time since I have had such good champagne," someone said still smacking his lips. Sitting next to her was a young prostitute who exchanged her body with the men around her for bread. In Russia, almost all of these people were professors or experts of some sort. One of them recited a poem of Wang Wei in Chinese and another quoted Aristotle in Greek.

As the night ended, O bought a prop from *The Lower Depths* for two thousand francs. It was a cloak assembled from materials picked out of the trash. O held it in her arms and paced the room while telling us the last part of this story. When she left, they did not want to let her go. They were charmed by her pre-October Revolution aristocratic accent. They hoped she would come again and, if possible, bring a few more bottles of champagne. As she was talking, she tossed the cloak over her shoulders, like an ancient Russian sprite.

9

PARIS IS A DIFFICULT CITY to describe and those bold enough to try are most likely tourists. Tour guides lead them around by their noses like cows, and since time is short and they usually don't know French, there is little chance for them to range freely. Tourism is in the process of becoming a man-made disaster. Travel culture is more virulent than infectious diseases such as hoof-and-mouth disease. Like some kind of sleight of hand, it turns the false into the real, history into present reality, tourists into residents, day into night, tears into laughter, and vice versa. Travel these days is somewhat similar to the train hopping we took part in as students during the Cultural Revolution when all the schools were shut down, except here capital pulls the strings behind the scenes. This thing, capital, can't be seen or touched, but it gives one heartburn nonetheless. They say that if China becomes a bourgeois society, and everyone decides to make a trip to Paris, the city will be host to an extra twenty million tourists every day.

I set out from my house, walked by the Pompidou, crossed the Seine, and passed through the city within a city, the Île de la Cité, to the Left Bank's Latin Quarter. Like Beijing, Paris is an imperial city, but it is more similar to Shanghai.

In reality, people aren't very different from dogs and also rely primarily on their noses to live. In the depths of memory, smells are more enduring than images. Proust writes: ". . . after the death of people, after the destruction of things, alone, frailer but more enduring, more immaterial, more persistent, more faithful, smell and taste still remain for a long time, like souls, remembering, waiting, hoping, upon the ruins of all the rest, bearing without giving way, on their almost impalpable droplet, the immense edifice of memory." Having lived overseas for a long time, my memories of home have become more cloudy and more abstract, but the unique smells of Beijing come back to me from time to time: the sharp, mildewy smell of cabbages stored away for the winter, the thick smoke of charcoal stoves, the freshness of elm trees in bloom, the fishy stench of lake waters in the summer, the reek of urine in narrow alleyways, the spicy odor of mutton roasting on skewers. The smells of Paris are totally different: coffee wafting everywhere, the cloying scent of roasting chestnuts, winter leaves in the rain, the dizzying effect of women's perfume, the alcoholic stench of the homeless in the metro.

Over the past couple of days Y has told me again and again that he was trained as a painter, and now he wants to buy a roomy apartment and take up his brushes again. Someday he won't be able to photograph purses any more, and so he will support himself by painting. Whenever he gets on this subject, he waves his fists in excitement, urging himself on. He also refuses to admit the reality of his exile status, otherwise he thinks he will grow old and wither away.

10

AFTER M GRADUATED FROM THE Chinese department of Beijing University, he was first sent to a district party school, and then transferred to a certain editorial division. In 1984, he edited an internal party publication called *An Anthology of New Trends in Poetry*. This set of books had a profound and wide-reaching influence. Almost immediately after publication, the poets associated with *Today* received public recognition.

I met M shortly after the anthology was published. He lived on the third floor of a dormitory for unmarried students at the local party school—an ugly, oppressive building, dim and dark, full of the odor of dust. His father was a railroad worker and lived in a remote mountain valley in Hunan. I think trains brought him childhood dreams, and eventually brought him to the distant north. He was small, his head round, and his plastic glasses were held together with tape. He spoke quickly, his words piling on top of each other, and sometimes he would suddenly blush.

At the end of 1988, I went back to Beijing from England. My new place was very close to his work unit and dormitory, and he often came to see me. At my house, we drafted the February 1989 petition to the government for the release of Wei Jingsheng and others. Thirty of us signed it. Three months later, I traveled to San Francisco for a meeting. At that time, the student movement had just begun, and my heart was not in the meeting. Every day, my eyes were fixed on the developments of the situation at home. When I heard that M was the head of the publicity department of the Tiananmen student association, a cold sweat poured over me. After the guns started to fire, he fled with the head of the security team and disappeared for several months. He finally resurfaced in Paris, where he received a welcome fit for a hero of the people.

In the spring of 1990, a number of us held a meeting in Oslo where we decided to start publishing *Today* again. M rushed north from Paris to join us. At the reunion, everyone was very emotional, but we quickly discovered that we had become strangers to each other. M still lived in a state of excitement, and his thinking was as muddy as his vision. He brought a form with him, planning to enroll all the writers as members of his "Democratic Front." When he spoke about how impressive he had been on the square, with his bodyguards thronging around him, he narrowed his eyes, basking in self-satisfaction. But the piece he wrote for the new issue of *Today* was nothing but empty slogans. I know that he still suffers. He says that I have betrayed the revolution.

When I came to Paris in early 1991, M invited me along with a few other friends to a gathering that was held at his Taiwanese girlfriend's place. The party ended on a sour note. Not long before, the French newspaper *Libération* had interviewed M, in the course of which M said some things that should not have been said. At the party, he was severely berated for this by some of the other guests, and he began bawling. When I left him in the early morning, his face was still covered with tears.

After that, I only caught a glimpse of him on the metro. I didn't say anything to him—just watched his stocky outline disappear into the boundless sea of people. News of him was sporadic. He became the chairman of the Paris arm of the "Democratic Front," and was later unseated in an election but was unwilling to hand over the reins. His girlfriend broke up with him and he was cast out onto the streets of Paris. Constantly borrowing money from friends, a few of them finally rented an apartment for him. But he played loud music at all hours and flooded the floor when he bathed. The landlord booted him out after only a few days. Then for many years there was no news of him. It was said that he had drifted to Rome and then returned to Paris again. Maybe someday I will run into him on the streets of Paris.

In a brief ten years, he went from the high valleys of

Hunan to Beijing University to Tiananmen Square to Paris. He began with the makings of a strong poetry critic and editor, but the simple country boy was swept away in the tide of revolution, and in the end it drove him mad. And now that I think about it, I'm partly to blame.

II

BOSS L WAS NOT VERY TALL, his shoulders were sloped, and he had a shiny red face. His whiskers and hair were turning white, making him look like he had just come in from a blizzard. His eyes narrowed to a crack, often causing a smile behind his glasses. Boss L was a prominent figure in Paris's Chinese cultural circle. The restaurant he ran was considered a landmark in Paris and was well-known abroad, primarily because of the proprietor's enthusiasm for culture: "He had erudite scholars to converse with, and no dealings with the common man." And he loved to play the host. Every year at Mid-Autumn Festival, he hosted a crabmeat banquet with more than one hundred guests. Any Chinese person passing through Paris, as long as they had the slightest bit of culture around the edges, could look forward to being waited on by him at least once; it was like he was waiting on Chinese culture itself. How could he have known that for most writers and artists, their work has nothing to do with culture, but is merely a way to put food on the table.

Boss L was from Wenzhou. He lost his mother when he was young and was raised by his father. He finished high school in Hong Kong and then ran away to Paris to seek his fortune, first as a cook, then as a restaurateur. His wife was

also his cousin, so they were related by both blood and affection, the husband setting the tune and the wife harmonizing.
For some time, their business boomed. His life, originally, was
no different from that of any other restaurant owner, but the
Tiananmen crackdown changed him. When he heard that the
government had opened fire, he boiled over with rage. Immediately, he quit gambling so that he could put time and
money into the overseas democracy movement. But the tide
of the democracy movement ebbed after a few years, with
some people splitting off and others departing altogether,
leaving him stranded. Lost and alone, he became acquainted
with a band of Chinese people who remained behind in Paris
and were active in the cultural scene. It was quite unexpected
that L would be so enraptured by culture. Because of his new
cultural ambitions, he spent all his free time with friends
talking about any issue under the sun. The restaurant went
into decline and his wife did not voice her dissatisfaction—she
simply left him.

On the night before the New Year, we got together at a
friend's place. Everyone was drunk except L. In the early
hours of the morning, he drove me home. Paris was full of
people waiting for their rides, surging across the streets like a
tide. He handled the steering wheel deftly, swerving by people
hailing cabs. Where was the other shore in this endless sea of
night? Our conversation turned, and he heaved a long sigh,
"What kind of thing is life, do you think? In just one night
wealth lost its interest for me, and at my age I suddenly can
follow a different road, live a new way . . ."

Whenever we met up, Boss L always had to wait for the
restaurant to close before driving over with a couple bottles of
good French wine. He'd come in, greet us, sit down, then taste
the food and give the obligatory critique. He has been hang-

ing out in the same cultural circle for a decade and is amazingly adept at bringing people together through his social connections. Sometimes, when he meets a newly arrived master of the game, he grows silent, sips his wine, and grins.

12

I CALLED S IN SINGAPORE. A Philippine maid told me in English, "The master is sleeping," which annoyed me. When did he become "master"? "Go wake him up," I replied. "I dare not," mumbled the maid.

Fifteen years ago, S came to Beijing for a meeting and he stopped by. At the time he was a handsome and quiet young man—both arrogant and modest. After Tiananmen, he became the "criminal mastermind" of the Shanghai student movement and was sent to jail in chains. Just before he was sentenced, he wrote a "Letter on Descending into Hell," full of the righteous feeling of youth. This document was passed around and made it overseas and was published in *Today*. He won the 1992 Rotterdam international poetry festival prize in the imprisoned poets category. Because the news was never made public in China, a Romanian poet (who had also been in prison) accepted the award for him. S, who had recently been released, was riding a bicycle in and out of the narrow alleys of Shanghai, oblivious of having won the award.

Soon after, he fell in love with Lili, a French girl, and moved to Paris. Lili had some Chinese blood in her and could speak Chinese. I returned to Paris in the spring of 1993, just in time for their wedding banquet. Lili's friends, family, teachers, and classmates were there, clouds filling the sky, proving the health of Parisian social networks. But there were only drinking buddies on the groom's side, making clear the embarrassing circumstances of this Asian drifter.

S was a poet in the truest sense. Most poets put on a show of threatening bravado, bearing their fangs and hinting at dark intentions. His subdued and gentle elegance was uncommon. He listened intently to others with his melancholy eyes focused on them, and he spoke like a somnambulist, as if trying to correct reality with dream.

Not long after their marriage, they had a son. The pressures of life forced Lili to abandon her doctorate and start teaching high school. S studied French and at the same time taught Chinese to earn a little extra money. He began to lose his hair, hunch over, and grow distracted. I was living in the Netherlands at the time. One day I opened a piece of mail from him, but the envelope was empty. I rushed to Paris, and invited him to meet me at a coffee shop. We sat there drinking beer from afternoon until nightfall. His gaze was unfocused, his mood dejected, and it looked like he might slip off his chair at any moment. I tried to encourage him, knowing it was of no use. An artist or intellectual who has inherited one ancient tradition has a difficult time living in another. Even more serious than practical pressures is the sort of internal conflict that it produces—the two traditions are incompatible with each other.

When I saw him next, his spirits had greatly improved. Like a badger emerging from hibernation, his eyes glittered. He had written a suite of poems about Paris, doubtless among his best work. Yes, he definitely was correcting the real with dream.

Lili found an overseas position in the French state department and the whole family was moving to Singapore for a few years. While I was happy about the good news, I was also worried: How would S get enough oxygen in that fishbowl of a city? He'd be entering another exile, away from his second home.

On reflection, I see that there must always be a correspondence between Paris and the Chinese poet: the difference of one meets the tolerance of the other; the solitary shadow and the source of light; the one's dream and the other's time; the foreign sensibility and the local accent; Chinese characters and streets that radiate out like the rays of a star.

13

Y SNEEZED TWICE IN MY FACE. He was exhausted from photographing purses, and he looked like he hadn't slept for days. He announced that, starting today, he was not going to work for two months and would fight his battles on the chessboard. I had arrived just in time for lunch. With a few deft motions, Y produced three dishes and a soup. After lunch, I took a nap and he reclined on the other bed to read the newspaper. He was soon snoring. Y is a mysterious man; I have no idea what he thinks about. He refuses the constraints of time, and also refuses affection. When I last took him to the airport, he was anxious and distracted. He stuffed a wallet into my hands like he had committed a crime. It turned out to be a gift.

I went out for a walk. Crossing the Pont Neuf, I couldn't help looking over the side of the bridge into the river. Many years earlier, an American writer friend came to Paris and we took our children to the Luxembourg Gardens. My daughter,

Tiantian, was eight then, a few years older than his child. Walking across the bridge, I mentioned the fact that Paul Celan had committed suicide by jumping off this bridge into the Seine. The children's eyes widened in fear and they asked what suicide was. Later this friend told me that his son had bothered him for a long time with this question. He couldn't figure out why a person would want to kill himself.

I crossed the bridge, turned a corner, and returned to the square of Notre Dame de Paris. A great wave of pigeons rolled over the heads of the tourists and settled in the square. An unruly child tried to chase them away. No. That was a scene from my memory. It was from thirteen years earlier, when I first brought Tiantian here. Utterly rapt, she was feeding bread to the pigeons. I adjusted my camera lens and snapped a photo. An unruly child rushed toward the pigeons, startling them into flight. They filled the air around us. Tiantian frowned; the wind lifted her blue jacket covered in multicolored dots. This instant was preserved, Notre Dame in the background.

Pigeons have their own vantage point, always looking down from the roofs of Paris. Dogs also have their own vantage point, but what they see is mostly paving stones and the moving feet of pedestrians. Mosquitoes have a mosquito's point of view, slipping in through a window and penetrating deep into human living spaces until they taste blood.

I suddenly thought of a fragment of Walter Benjamin's: "Old maps—in love, most people seek an eternal home. But there are also a few others who seek eternal wandering. The latter kind of people belong to the melancholic." I remembered the spring of 1991, when I was answering questions after a reading at the Pompidou Center. The emcee of the program asked me if I liked Paris. I said that I liked drifting, and that I didn't prefer any one place my road has passed through. My response disappointed him. In the eyes of the French, Paris is the ultimate, the unsurpassable. After the reading, Y came over with his girlfriend to get his book autographed. I turned and, taking him for one of the photographers, pulled him with me out of the hall down to the restaurant. Fortunately, he wasn't startled with this unexpected development, making the best of my mistake.

KAFKA'S PRAGUE

I

MICHAEL TOLD ME ON THE PHONE, "Don't worry, somebody will be there to pick you up. He's really tall, like a basketball player. . . ." Sure enough, as soon as I came out of customs I saw him holding a sign up in the air, his head bobbing above the crowd. He was very tall and skinny; his smiling face looked tired, but warm. His name was Stanislav, a musician who was also the chauffer for the Prague Writers' Festival. His English was not very good and he asked me if I spoke German. I said I didn't. He said that he was going to Germany at the end of the month to perform. I asked what instrument he played. He said something in German, and pantomimed with his hands. Piano? No. Pipe organ? He nodded emphatically. I asked him where he usually performed. He said usually for sick people. In a hospital? No. In a convalescent home? He nodded his head emphatically again. As long as it isn't a funeral home, I thought to myself. I abandoned my curiosity about two of the greatest details of his life, and looked out the window at the scenery.

I was in Berlin in the summer of 1989. Michael and his wife set out from Oslo, picked me up, and we drove through East Germany into Czechoslovakia. After crossing the border, we had lunch at the first city we entered. The waitress couldn't speak English, so with gestures and a few words of Russian, we ordered colas and Hungarian beef soup. We were happy when the bill came as the meal was virtually free. This was the first time I experienced the Western tourist's sense of superiority.

When we crossed the bridge across the Vltava River and entered downtown Prague, it was already dark. We parked the car on a bustling street and Michael gave me the telephone number of a sinologist named Olga. When I called, Olga's husband said that she was vacationing with their children in the country, but he welcomed us to stay at their house anyway. He was an architect and knew Prague like the back of his hand. We went out that night to have some drinks and wander around. He took us to Kafka's home beside the square of the Old Town, and pointed out that beneath our feet flowed a huge vein of ore. Prague's beauty is unique, especially at night. The ancient streetlamps lead wanderers into darkness until all sense of direction is lost. Under the light of the lamps, shadows turn and echoes rise and fall. I suddenly realized that Kafka's fiction is like this reality, a reality that can be touched.

It was the eve of the Velvet Revolution. I was introduced to Martin, who was Olga's colleague at the university and an editor of the underground literary journal, *Kritická Príloha* (*Revolver Revue*). At the time, he was busy secretly circulating a petition in support of the nephew of the former king, restoring the monarchy. He wanted us to sign it, but I'm not a fan of monarchies, so I refused.

Four years later, the *Revolver Revue* invited the European editor of *Today* and Professor Leo Ou-fan Lee from Harvard to hold a symposium in Prague. After eight or nine years, one of

these underground publications enjoyed a well-earned reputation, while the other was totally discredited. On the eve of
our departure, our hosts organized a poetry reading for us in
a medieval cellar. Afterward, an angel appeared. Martin introduced us: "This is the editor-in-chief of the *Revolver Revue*."
She gracefully sat down at our table, causing a disturbance
in the Chinese literary world. Leo Ou-fan Lee, his forehead
shining, lavished high praise on Czech dramatists; Zhang Ji,
clutching a cigarette, violently attacked the incursions of
American cultural hegemony; and I am certain that whatever
I said was utterly incoherent.

The third time I visited Prague was in the spring of 1995. I
was living in Paris at the time, and in response to Michael's
insistence, I took part in the Prague Writers' Festival at my
own expense. Michael is from New York, but he moved to
London in search of his spiritual home, got married, had children, and was trapped there for more than twenty years.
There was no room for him in the conservative world of English poetry. He was like a Kafka in London. In 1991, he organized the first Prague Writers' Festival. At the time, Michael
was the lackey of an English company that hosted the annual
Prague International Book Fair, with the Writers' Festival in-
cidentally tacked on to it. It seemed just about everyone was
Michael's boss, arrogantly ordering him around, making him
spin like a top.

Michael always took me to discos to show me Prague's
younger generation, hoping we would also breathe in some of
that same youthful spirit. But the music rattled my insides so
much that I had trouble holding my drink. Michael was
going through a divorce and suffering at the hands of the English merchants. Under the flashing lights, his face was
mournful. I called him "my successful friend," which suc-

ceeded in cheering him up a little. In a thick English accent, he laughed, "Me, mother-fucking successful? Successful my arse!"

2

KAFKA WAS BORN IN A building on the square of Prague's Old Town on July 3, 1883. He moved several times, but never far from the city of his birth. His Hebrew teacher recalled him saying, "Here was my secondary school, over there in that building facing us was the university, and a little further to the left, my office. My whole life—" and he drew a few small circles with his finger "—is confined to this small circle."

The building where Kafka was born was destroyed by a great fire in 1889. When it was rebuilt in 1902, only a part of it was preserved. In 1995, a bust of Kafka was set into the building's outer wall. A portent of the Prague Spring, Kafka was finally recognized by the Czech communist authorities, hailed as a "revolutionary critic of capitalist alienation."

During the first year of Kafka's life, his father, Hermann Kafka, opened a small general store on the north side of the old town square, first dealing in retail and later in wholesale. Kafka wrote in an unmailed letter to his father, "But since you gradually began to terrify me on all sides, and the shop and you became inseparable for me, the shop was no longer a pleasant place for me to be. Things which had at first been a matter of course for me began to torment and shame me, especially your treatment of the staff. . . . You I heard and saw screaming, cursing and raging in the shop, in a manner that, in my opinion at the time, had no equal anywhere in the world."

In another letter to his father, he wrote, "You could, for instance, rail at the Czechs, then at the Germans, then at the Jews, and not only selectively but in every respect, and finally no one was left but you. For me, you took on that enigmatic something that all tyrants have whose law is founded in their person, not their reasoning."

Between 1889 and 1893, when the family moved to a building called "At the Minute," Kafka's three sisters were born. These sisters eventually perished in Nazi concentration camps. Kafka went to a German elementary school. Many years later, in a letter to a friend, he described the following incident from his childhood: "Once, as a small boy, I received a sixpence and wanted very much to give it to an old beggar woman who was sitting between Old Town Square and Small Square. Now, this seemed to me an outrageous sum, a sum which most likely had never been given a beggar before, and I felt embarrassed in front of the woman to be doing something so outrageous, so I changed the sixpence and gave the woman a penny, walked around the entire complex of the Town Hall and the arcade along the Small Square, reappeared from the left as a completely new do-gooder, gave the woman another penny, started again to walk and happily did this ten times (or perhaps a little less, for I believe the woman later lost patience and left). In any case, in the end I was so exhausted, morally too, that I went home right away and cried until my mother replaced the sixpence."

In another letter to the same friend, Kafka relates the details of how he walked to school every morning: "Our cook, a small, dry, skinny, sharp-nosed, hollow-cheeked, yellowish yet firm, energetic, and superior woman, led me to school each morning. . . . Upon leaving the house the cook would say that she was going to tell the teacher how bad I'd been at home. . . . School itself was already a horror, and now the cook wanted to make it even more difficult for me. I would begin to plead, she would shake her head; the more I pleaded, the more I felt what I was pleading for to be of value, the greater the danger; I would stand still and beg for forgiveness, she dragged me along; I would threaten her with retaliation through my parents, she laughed, here she was almighty; I held on to the doorframes of the shops, on to the corner-stones, I didn't want to go on until she had forgiven me, I tore her back by her skirt (she didn't have it easy either), but she dragged me further, assuring me that even this she was going to report to the teacher; it would get late, the clock of the Church of St. James struck 8:00, you could hear the school bells, other children began to run, I was always most afraid of being late, by now we would have to run as well and always the thought, 'She's going to tell, she's not going to tell'; as it happened, she did not tell, ever, but she always had the op-portunity, and a seemingly increasing one (yesterday I did not tell, but today I will for sure), and from that she never de-sisted. And sometimes—think of it, Milena—she would stamp her feet in anger at me in the lane and a coal merchant was sometimes around and would watch us. Milena, what foolish-ness, and how I belong to you with all the cooks and threats and all that enormous amount of dust that thirty-eight years has whirled up and which has settled in my lungs."

3

THE GUEST HOUSE OF A certain ministry is near the Old Town Square, and when I came to Prague in 1995, this was where I stayed. The rooms were tolerably clean, the furniture old and solid, and the longest long-distance call you could make was to the desk downstairs; it recalled the socialist years before the Velvet Revolution. The old doorkeeper was clearly a relic of that era, sleepy-eyed and wearing the smiling face of a transitional period.

I hurriedly washed up and went downstairs to the lobby where Stanislav was waiting for me. Once again, we had a difficult time making ourselves understood. He gestured, where do you want to go, and I nodded and said, yes, yes. While walking through the Old Town Square, he stopped and, with his face full of awe, whispered, "There is Josef Skvorecky." All I knew about him was that he was a Czech novelist who lived in Canada and with whom I was supposed to read on Thursday evening. I was led to City Hall and I showed my invitation. When I went inside, I was stunned to see everyone else dressed in formal attire—the men in suits and leather shoes, the women all made-up and in long dresses. I was the only unkempt and ragged one there in my leather jacket, blue jeans, and tennis shoes, with a big book bag still slung over my shoulder. I looked like a refugee. But there was no place to run, no place to hide, nothing but to brace myself and head up to the third floor auditorium. City Hall is one of the historic sights of Prague, dating back to the thirteenth century. How many changes of rule has it witnessed over the past seven hundred years? How many lives and deaths?

His honor the mayor spoke first in fluent English. He kidded Michael about his short stature. Michael joked back, throwing in a reference to his recent collection of poems, *Disappearance*. Disappearance. What a good topic in this age of exhibition where not many people understand all its implications. At Michael's side was his girlfriend, Vlasta, the vice-chair of the Writers' Festival, a warm and outgoing woman in her forties. Michael mentioned the Czech poet Jaroslav Seifert. The evening's reading was in his memory. Michael raised his face and closed his eyes as he spoke, as though nostalgic for lost poems and the dead.

I enjoyed strolling the streets of Prague. Going back and forth between the reception center and the theater, I had to pass through the Old Town Square. It was the night before Easter and tourists surrounded the open-air stages; vendors were selling colored eggs, traditional wooden toys, and crystal at their stalls. I went into a clothing store and transformed myself into a real pillar of society for the nightly receptions at the various embassies so that I would not become a public disgrace again. Compared to five years earlier, Prague had changed quite a bit. It was becoming more commercialized, and there were advertisements everywhere for the name-brand products of multinational corporations. One could also see that the Czech people maintained a certain self-confidence that kept them from being totally consumed by the battering waves of commercialism. The streets were full of dazzling Czech girls. They have an unworldly beauty that you don't usually see in the U.S. or Western Europe, a kind of earthy beauty often extinguished by modernization.

It surprised me to find so many young Americans living in Prague, enough for them to have their own newspaper. Michael explained, "The cost of living is so low here they can escape the pressures of American life. And Prague is like Paris in the '30s, so some come here for artistic inspiration." Shaking his head, he added, "But why haven't I seen anyone get anywhere with it?"

Michael took me to see his new house. As we left the tourist district, there were fewer people on the streets.

Michael was carrying a pile of books in his arms and, as if in a dream, said as he walked, "Look, the only one in this world who loves me is Vlasta. . . . I've found no one else in Prague who I can get into a deep conversation with. Everything is superficial, shiny, feigned happiness. . . . Most Czech writers are nationalists and they don't like it that a foreigner is running the Writers' Festival. No matter where I go, I am a foreigner. And the English are worse, snobbish conservatives convinced of their own correctness. New York used to be my home, but my home doesn't exist any more. . . ."

Every morning there was a press conference for the Writers' Festival at the Globe Bookstore. Most of the books sold there were in English, and there was a coffee shop inside. Several computers lined the wall, available for customers to check their e-mail. There were no chairs, so customers had to perch like birds, unable to settle in and refuse to leave. I headed over to a computer thinking I might catch up a little on this new age, but I didn't know how to use it. I asked the young fellow sitting next to me and he deftly used the cursor to lead me into the labyrinth. But as soon as he left me alone, the screen froze and I instantly broke into a cold sweat.

A man draped in cameras greeted me. He introduced himself as Rossano, the designated photographer for the Writers' Festival. His head was covered with ruffled hair, and his eyes were as shiny as his camera lenses. I followed him into the street. Rossano had a unique way of taking pictures, either making me stand on a stone block in front of a church like a martyr, or enclosing me in a telephone kiosk like a prisoner. He came from Florence, and was a typical Italian—warm and hearty. "Why do you live in Prague?" I asked him. "Simple. I married a girl from Prague and we just had a child," he sighed.

The press conference was about to end. The coffee shop was filled with people. Susan Sontag sat at the rostrum, handling the various maneuvers of the reporters' questions that ranged from the war in Kosovo to globalization. She had just gotten off the airplane, but there seemed to be no sign of fatigue at all, her words were sharp-edged, and she had the courage of her convictions. I waited until Michael announced that the press conference was over and walked over to greet Susan. She brushed away a lock of white hair that had slipped down onto her forehead. We agreed to meet for dinner to talk—no reporters, no interviews, no cameras.

4

Prague isn't willing to leave, nor will it let us leave. This girl has claws, and people must line up, or we will have to light a fire at Vysehrad and the Old Town Square before we can possibly depart.

—Excerpt from a letter from Kafka to Oskar Pollak

CHARLES UNIVERSITY WAS ESTABLISHED in 1348—the oldest university in Central Europe. In 1882 it was divided into a German university and a Czech university. Kafka enrolled in the German university in 1901, his academic performance mediocre. For him, studying law was simply a matter of expedience since Jews could only pursue professional degrees such as medicine and law.

In a letter to a friend, he described his first sexual experience: "We were living in Zeltnergasse at that time. Opposite was a clothes shop, a shopgirl was always standing in the doorway. I was little over the age of twenty, ceaselessly pacing back and forth in my room, preoccupied with the nerve-racking rote-learning of what I considered to be senseless things for the first state exam. It was summer, very hot at this time I guess, it was absolutely unbearable, at the window I remained, the disgusting Roman Law History between my teeth, always standing. Finally, we communicated through signs. I was to fetch her at eight o'clock in the evening, but when I went down, another was already there, well, that did not change a lot, I was afraid of the entire world, and also of this man; had he not been there, I would still have been afraid of him. But though the girl slipped her arm through his, she gave me a sign that I should follow them. Thus we came to Schützeninsel, drank beer there, I at the neighboring table, then we slowly walked, with me behind, to the girl's flat, somewhere around the Fleischmarkt. There the man took his leave, the girl disappeared into the house, I waited for a bit until she came out again, and then we went to a hotel on the Kleinseite. All that was charming, exciting, and disgusting, even before the hotel, and in the hotel it was no different.

And when, towards morning, it was still hot and beautiful, we went back home over the Charles Bridge, I was, of course, happy, but this happiness meant only that my eternally moaning body had finally found relief, but most of all, this happiness consisted of the fact that the whole thing had not been even more disgusting, even dirtier."

In the winter of 1904, the twenty-one-year-old Kafka began to write the first draft of *Description of a Struggle*. In a letter to a friend from that time, he wrote, "A book must be the ax for the frozen sea within us. I believe that." In this book, I—the narrator—describes his night ramblings with a classmate through a cold and bleak Prague. But his other books are not like this one, where Prague plays such a central role. The famous landmarks Kafka touches on in the course of these midnight rambles are still there with the exception of a few that were destroyed in the Second World War.

The Charles Bridge is the oldest and most famous bridge in Prague, crossing the Vltava River, linking the Old Town with the opposite bank. This bridge's predecessor was destroyed by floodwaters and ice floes. In 1357, Charles IV instructed his architects to build the Charles Bridge. Except for two arches damaged in a flood in 1890, it has miraculously survived wars and disasters down to the present day.

In the diary entry for June 19, 1919, Kafka wrote, "With Ottla. She is fetched by her English teacher. Over the quay, stone bridge, small piece of Mala Strana, new bridge, home. Exciting statues of saints on Charles Bridge. The odd evening light of summertime when the bridge is deserted at night."

In a letter to a friend, he wrote: "There is within everyone a devil which gnaws the nights to destruction, and that is neither good nor bad, rather, it is life: if you did not have it, you could not live. So what you curse in yourself is your life. This devil is the material (and a fundamentally wonderful one) which you have been given and which you must now make use of. . . . On the Charles Bridge in Prague, there is a relief under the statue of a saint, which tells your story. The saint is ploughing a field there and has harnessed a devil to the plough. Of course, the devil is still furious (hence the transitional stage; as long as the devil is not satisfied the victory is not complete), he bares his teeth, looks back at his master with a crooked, nasty expression and convulsively retracts his tail; nevertheless, he is submitted to the yoke. . . ."

5

I WAS STANDING IN FRONT of the French windows of the Mlynec Restaurant, gazing out at the glowing Charles Bridge. The coffee shop was too extravagant, too nouveau riche. I was reading an English edition of *Franz Kafka and Prague* by Harald Salfellner. The back cover of the book cites the words of Kafka's friend Johannes Urzidil: "Kafka was Prague, and Prague was Kafka. It was never so wholly and typically Prague, and would never again be as it was in Kafka's lifetime. And we, his friends, 'the happy few,' . . . we knew that this Prague is contained in the smallest quanta everywhere in his works."

The Prague Writers' Festival went smoothly. Writers ascended to and descended from the podium one after another, the applause from the audience rose and fell, the theater filled and emptied. If Kafka had been alive, he would certainly have found the Writers' Festival absurd, and perhaps he would have written a story about it. Today's entire activity is called "Prague" and all the writers are Czech—except for me. In the evening, Josef Skvorecky and I will share the stage for a reading. How did I get placed in the ranks of the Czech writers? It was Michael's idea. He said he had originally planned to have me read with Vaclav Havel, and to do this he went right over to the presidential residence; but Havel's advisor sent him away with the excuse that he did not understand English. The fortress refused invitations from another world.

In the afternoon, I was interviewed on the national television station. The host of the program told me that in 1968, after Soviet troops had occupied Prague, this studio number nine, due to its isolated location, still kept up the cry of resistance. It took the Russians two days to find it.

There was not an empty seat in the house that evening. The audience had come to see Skvorecky, who enjoyed even more fame in the Czech Republic than Milan Kundera. In 1968, not long after the Soviet invasion, Skvorecky fled to Toronto, began teaching at a university there, and assisted his wife in setting up the 68 Publishers, which specialized in banned books by Czech authors. A Czech scholar told me that after Skvorecky fled he still made a great contribution to the Czech cause, but Kundera has always disdained his homeland and identified himself as French.

Skvorecky had caught a bad cold and was sitting at the rear podium drinking brandy. He had gotten old, he said to me, and wasn't fit for traveling long distances. Then he went to the podium, still drinking brandy, and read his story "Bass Saxophone," first in his native language, then in English. Applause thundered, someone shouted something in a loud voice, and the Czech people saluted their hero. It was my turn to read for the second half, but first Michael gave a brief introduction. He closed his eyes as though thinking about the past.

My "date" the previous evening with Susan Sontag had been bruited around, causing quite a stir. Susan was too famous, cold as an icebox, and had an aura of mystery. Rossano asked me to try to work out a photo op for him; the undersecretary at the Swedish consulate asked me to pass his business card to her, to give her his highest regards, and to tell her that he had adored her for many years. Entrusted with these important missions, I waited at the hotel where she was staying.

At 9:40, Susan finally returned from her television interview. "Oh, all the stupid questions, it was torture. Let's go, I'm starving."

We took a taxi to a Chinese restaurant. I noticed that the driver hadn't turned on the meter and was circling the city on his way to the restaurant. When we got to our destination, he asked for a fare more than three times higher than it should have been. I signaled to Susan to get out of the car first, stuffing half the fare that he was asking for into his hands. He began cursing me in Czech, but fortunately I didn't understand him.

At the dinner table, I passed on the Italian's request and the Swede's admiration. Susan took the business card and sighed. "Whenever I accept an invitation, I always forget about the media and their endless questions."

When I brought up Havel, Susan said that many Czechs criticized him but she always spoke up for him. When she last visited Prague, Havel had invited her to a tête-à-tête dinner in a restaurant, but his bodyguards were seated nearby. She had wanted to ask him his real feelings about a number of things. "You know, under those circumstances, I couldn't bring myself to ask them."

I replied, "What I don't understand is, as a writer, how can he tolerate that kind of life? It isn't much better than being in jail. For example, he can't just walk down the street anymore, or talk with ordinary people."

At midnight, we took a walk down the street, neon signs representing the Western world flirted with the Prague night. Susan suddenly said, "That's right, nobody wants to bring back the old system, but could it be that this emptiness is what they want?" I suggested that we have another drink. We turned into a bar, ordered two beers, and talked some more. I spoke about my daughter, American schools, and the problems of today's youth; Susan spoke about her son who was studying history—he was her best friend in the world.

Walking Susan back to her hotel, the streetlamps of Prague made us lose our way.

MIDNIGHT'S GATE

Knowledge of death is the only key that can open midnight's gate.

AT 3:30 P.M. ON MARCH 24, 2002, Air France flight 1992 arrived at Tel Aviv International Airport. We took a shuttle to the entrance of the customs inspection area and crowded together in line. An official from the Israeli foreign affairs office unexpectedly burst in, collected all our passports, disappeared, and then reappeared; we filed out after him through a special exit. I had just breathed a sigh of relief when I was stopped by a muscular young man who was clearly a plainclothes police officer. He said that for security purposes, I had to answer some questions truthfully. The purpose of my trip? I mumbled that I was a member of the International Parliament of Writers delegation. He heard "delegation" as "interrogation." What? International Writers' Interrogation? His ears pricked up. No, not interrogation, I hurriedly waved my hand to call over our Secretary General, Salmon. But Salmon only spoke French, and the three of us grew more confused as we tried to speak, unable to figure out just who was interrogating whom. Fortunately, the representative of the French Consulate in Israel who was supposed to pick us up made a timely appearance and finally broke the siege. The plainclothes policeman, tapping two fingers to his temple, said goodbye to us in French.

There were eight members of the International Parliament of Writers delegation representing eight countries and four continents. Besides the chair, our group included: the American novelist Russell Banks; the South African poet Breyten Breytenbach; the Italian novelist Vincenzo Consolo; the Spanish novelist Juan Goytisolo; the Secretary General of the International Parliament of Writers Christian Salmon; the Portuguese novelist José Saramago; the Nigerian poet and dramatist Wole Soyinka; and myself. At six o'clock the previous evening, we'd held a press conference at the France Television booth in the main hall of the Paris Book Fair where we presented the "Call for Peace in Palestine" signed by over five hundred writers from more than thirty countries, including several Israeli writers.

Ten or so reporters joined us, and at the airport gate we all got into a bus provided by the French Consulate. The highway stretched into the interior, the landscape becoming more and more desolate. This was a wasteland, with hills and mountains of sand and stone forming a bleak ocean, and shrubs and wild grass scattered here and there. It reminded me of the Gobi Desert.

In the spring of 1990, the Chinese poet Duo Duo and I took part in the International Poetry Festival in Jerusalem. We were ferried around in buses then, too. It had been an enormous transformation for us—in language, as well as in time and space. I remember Duo Duo swimming in the Dead Sea, and then regretting it as he crawled out of the water. Israel is a paramilitary state, and it was extremely common to see young men holding a gun in one hand and embracing a girlfriend in the other, strolling down the street as though it were the most natural thing in the world. When one brings up the Middle East crisis with Israeli writers, they are often dissatisfied with their right-wing politicians, but also power-less to do anything. When it comes to talking about the future, most of them simply shift their gaze, faces full of gloom. At the border between Israel and Syria, the kibbutzim reminded me of the military units set up on the Sino-Soviet border in the sixties and seventies.

Twelve years had gone by in a flash, from one year of the horse to the next. But this time I was headed for the other side of the border.

In the nineties, there were real prospects for peace. On September 13, 1993, Yitzhak Rabin and Yasser Arafat shook hands for the first time and signed the limited autonomy agreement. On September 28, 1995, they signed a second treaty, and Israel subsequently withdrew its army from the West Bank. That same year, these two men shared the Nobel Peace Prize. Arafat ended twenty-seven years of exile and re-turned to his homeland. But on November 4, 1995, Rabin's assassination by a right-wing extremist cast a shadow over the peace process. History is often influenced by random events. If the assassin had not succeeded, the arrow of time might have pointed in a different direction. A random event plucked George W. Bush and Ariel Sharon from the mass of humanity, letting them onto the political stage, bringing many changes to the world. And so the twenty-first century began with these changes.

The incandescent sun, hanging alone in the sky, closed in on the backs of our heads like the silent muzzle of a gun. An eagle wheeled above as if trying to spread its folded shadow over the earth. A sentry post loomed ahead. A soldier with a rifle inspected our vehicle's license plate and border pass. Machine guns stood on tripods on the sandbags of a nearby embankment. The road in the opposite direction was jammed

with vehicles. Our guide told me that it was absolutely forbid-
den for Palestinians to drive on this road. Our side was clear
because our destination was Ramallah, the besieged city from
which Arafat governed.

Gradually the sky darkened and the scenery changed—
from a sentry box beside a dark and gloomy military camp
with tanks, to a blockhouse, its embrasures like empty eye-
sockets. The door of our bus opened with a grating sound,
and the representative from the French Consulate, weilding a
special permit from the Israeli Ministry of Defense, negoti-
ated with the soldier. The cameraman followed him, his flash
constantly glaring. The soldier called his superior on a
walkie-talkie and asked him for instructions, then took away
our passports and climbed into our bus to check them one by
one. He was very young with tired, cold eyes. His face displayed a lack of affect that seemed to say, "You guys are just
asking for trouble—have you come here to die?" He contacted
his superior again on the walkie-talkie, waited a while, then
finally waved us on. The bus had not gone very far before
there was another sentry box, but this one didn't hold us up
so long. After we had continued on for a while, a Palestinian
police officer in blue camouflage appeared. He made a gesture, and a police car on the side of the road pulled out and
led the way for us, its blue roof-lights flashing. At last we
entered Ramallah.

In Arabic, "Ramallah" means "God's high place," though
actually the city isn't even nine hundred meters above sea
level. Situated on a hill sixteen kilometers north of Jerusalem,
it looks over the neighboring hills. With numerous springs, it
is a well-known summer retreat on the west bank of the Jordan River. Ramallah now refers to the two cities of Ramallah
and Al-Bireh. Ramallah was founded in the twelfth century

during the occupation of the Crusader armies, but the history of Al-Bireh can be traced back to the Canaanite period of 3500 B.C. Al-Bireh is mentioned in the Bible seventy-six times, and it is said the Virgin Mary often stayed here. The inhabitants of Ramallah used to be mostly Catholics, but after the War of 1948, there was a large influx of Palestinian refugees. In the 1950s, Ramallah belonged to Jordan. Then, during the Six-Day War of 1967, it fell into the hands of Israel. In 1988, Jordan returned sovereignty to the Palestinians of the West Bank, but in reality the territory was still governed by Israel. Not until 1996, when Israel withdrew its troops, did Ramallah become the capital of the Palestinian West Bank.

At night, Ramallah looks like a ghost town—no people on the streets, few cars, most of the buildings unlit. It was a quarter to seven when we arrived at the Grand Park Hotel. Our hosts were waiting at the door. Leading them was Mahmoud Darwish, the most famous Palestinian poet of the present generation. When a reporter asked about the purpose of our trip to Palestine, Soyinka answered it well: "It is very simple, we have accepted the invitation of our besieged colleague, the Palestinian poet Darwish. On two occasions, we all hoped he would be able to accept a certain prize from an American university and interact with other writers. This gathering was delayed due to the events of 1992, and then canceled. As I see it, it is a great pity that he lost this chance to cross over the borders. Since Darwish was unable to come to us, it was up to us to go to him. It is as simple as that."

The Garden Park Hotel was quite luxurious, its marble so polished it reflected your image, the staff faultlessly courteous. In besieged Ramallah, this contrast added to the surreal atmosphere. Darwish was wrapped in a piece of white silk, his age difficult to judge. Hardship generally hastens aging, but sometimes it can also erase the marks of time. He has an optimistic nose that makes him look like he's perpetually grinning. Born in 1941, he was seven when his village was attacked by Zionists. When Darwish fled to Lebanon, he was separated from his family and became an orphan. A year later, he returned home to find it reduced to ruins, an Israeli settlement in its place. He began to write poetry in elementary school, but because he failed his "political review," he could not go on to middle school. He has been imprisoned and put under house arrest numerous times.

We rested for a while and then walked together to a banquet given by the Palestinian Ministry of Culture. Outside, it was a bit cool, the moon had risen, everything cast in its pure light. In the distance, the lights of Jerusalem shined bright—that Holy City of three religions, the cause of so many disasters throughout history, all in the name of God. As an activity of the imagination, religion seems to arise from a fear of death and the unknown world. Unlike poetry, it arises from the collective imagination and of necessity forms a relationship with authority, then subsequently transforms into an authority, systematizes, and even militarizes, so that when it encounters another collective imagination, the clashing of swords and the flowing of blood inevitably follows. That religious warfare is nearly absent throughout the history of China is most likely because Buddhism and Daoism value individual religious experience and discourage the mixing of religion with other endeavors, so "Those on different paths don't make plans together," and if the road isn't clear, "Just stand on earth to attain Enlightenment." Furthermore, imagination requires space, and in the Middle East, especially in the Holy City, space is extremely limited. The dissemination and feedback of imagination always makes the situation more complex. For example, the first of the eight Crusades to the East was a failure. This particular image of the imagination was initially linked to a Pope's ambition to unite the Catholic and Eastern Orthodox Churches, which in turn aroused a hermit slumbering in a French monastery. By fanning the flames underground, kindling fires at the base level of society, he gathered eighty thousand poor peasants on the banks of the Rhine and set out for the East. Blind hatred and the promise of Heaven were the motives, yet they did not even know for sure where the Holy City was, nor did they have any supplies. They made their way south and east by robbing and looting and in the end were cruelly defeated by the Turks, fewer than three thousand surviving.

It was a buffet-style banquet. What most surprised me was the excellent local wine that we drank. Holding my glass of wine, I looked out the French doors at the night view of Ramallah. An elegant middle-aged woman walked up to me; her name was Tania. She said she was a soprano, an amateur; I said I was a poet, also an amateur. She laughed. She talked about her mother, her daily life under siege. She pointed to some buildings surrounded by a wall on a mountain, saying it was an Israeli settlement that was continually expanding and that Israeli soldiers often fired guns in this direction for no particular reason, resulting in the deaths of numerous children. Just a week ago, she said, the streets here were full of tanks. Darwish interrupted to say that there were 140 tanks in Ramallah. Tania practicing amidst the roar of tanks is an image that has haunted me ever since.

When I woke up the next morning, I didn't know where I was. A thread of sunlight slipped in from behind the curtain. I remembered going to the Israeli Consulate in San Francisco to get my visa, and a young Jewish man at the entrance ques-

tioned me. I said I was going to Palestine. He said there was
no Palestine. His tone of voice was calm, natural, with no hint
of doubt. At a glance I could tell that he had had a good up-
bringing, was good at heart, but had absolutely no awareness
of the tragedy he denied.

At breakfast, I ran into Juan, Vincenzo, and a Palestinian
professor. Juan asked if I wanted to walk with them downtown. He lives in Morocco and can speak a little Arabic. He
writes experimental novels and is a social activist, which
makes him a typical public intellectual. This role, quite common in Europe, has become almost extinct in the United
States. Juan travels all over the world and publishes articles in
large Spanish newspapers attacking the injustices of the
times, influencing the direction of public opinion. He once
traveled with a television production team to Palestine and
this professor had been their guide.

We took a taxi to the center of Ramallah. There was little
to distinguish it from a remote town in Xinjiang or South
Africa—poverty stricken, but bustling with life. Coca-Cola
and Motorola signs marked street crossings. Vendors cried
their wares at an open-air market spread out with fresh fruits
and vegetables. The professor greeted everyone on the street,
squeezed the fruit, tasted the medicinal herbs, asked prices,
or chatted about the weather. Juan bought a copy of the
International Herald Tribune at a newsstand. To my surprise,
this newsstand was stocked with all kinds of popular American magazines like *Life*, *Penthouse*, and *Seventeen*.

The professor showed us the shops and houses that had
been destroyed by Israeli fire, most of which had been repaired, though one could still make out the fresher color of
the recently repaired spots. Photo after photo was pasted on
the walls like the rosters of model workers we used to have

back home. Among the multitude of young men there was a beautiful girl. These were the "martyrs" who had blown themselves up. The professor told me that the girl had died only a month earlier, twenty-eight years old, the first female martyr.

We walked to the cultural center. Named after the Palestinian poet, educator, and social activist Khalil Sakakini, whose entire life was steeped in legend. During World War I, he went to jail for sheltering Polish Jews. The center was built in 1927 and used to be the residence of the mayor of Ramallah. We walked past a meticulously ordered garden and through an arched entryway. An exhibition of paintings was on the first floor, and the second story was all offices including the editorial department of the literary magazine of which Darwish was the editor-in-chief. The stairs led us to the third-floor conference room.

We sat facing the Palestinian writers. The members of our delegation were introduced by Leila Shahid, the official Palestinian representative in France. She was a rotund woman who liked to make jokes. Introducing Vincenzo Consolo, she first said his name with the accent on the first syllable, "*con*sole," like a television, a rather material rendition; then she shifted the accent, making it a verb, "con*sole*," which had a more spiritual quality. This was good: Mr. Consolation.

Darwish was the first to speak, and he began with a reference to "the bloody spring." He said, "Your courageous visit is a break in the siege. You make us feel that we are no longer alone. History has been too long with too many prophets. We understand that this space held in multiple embraces is not a prison, and that no one has a monopoly on a land, a god, or a memory. We also know that history is neither fair nor elegant. But our mission is to be human—we are both the sacrificial victims of history and its creation." He concluded, "And the incurable disease we suffer from is hope. . . . Hope will make this place regain its original meaning: a land of love and peace. Thank you for bearing the burden of hope with us."

Hope is a burden indeed. Three days later, the Israeli army again occupied Ramallah, as well as the greater part of the West Bank. Nor was the cultural center spared: the works of art and the offices were completely demolished, the computer hard drives removed.

After Darwish's speech, we attended a press conference held by the Palestine Media Center. Saramago was the center of attention because before leaving Paris, he had shocked everyone with his comment comparing the Israeli authorities to the Nazis, using words like "Auschwitz" and "Holocaust." Most of the members of the delegation were uneasy, fearing that his provocative language would affect the goal of our trip. I didn't feel Saramago had done anything wrong. After all, we are not politicians and have no need to use diplomatic rhetoric. A writer has the right to use metaphor. If he can alert society with it, this merely shows the efficacy of language. Furthermore, Saramago's words were prophetic, proven by the massacres that followed in Jinin and other places. Israel does not possess exclusive rights over words such as "Auschwitz" and "Holocaust." Past victims can also become today's tyrants. This is the darkness of human nature, the darkness of the cycle of vengeance, the darkness of hatred people sink into. And the writer is a traveler who passes through this darkness.

During the press conference, I mentioned that there is another siege, the siege of the language of hate. Juan, sitting to my left, said he agreed completely. Perhaps because Spain and China have had similar histories of censorship, language issues assume a heightened importance to us.

We had accepted an invitation from the president of Berzeit University to lunch with the professors. Berzeit University is in a northern suburb of Ramallah. The bus we were riding in suddenly stopped, impeded by a cement roadblock. We had to walk about five hundred meters and get into another car at the other end of the blocked-off section. I asked Tania why. She shrugged her shoulders and said, "They are just making life difficult for us." She told me the sentry posts had originally been set by the side of the road, then later moved up to the hillside. She pointed to a blockhouse on the hillside: "There are Israeli marksmen up there who can shoot anyone they don't like the look of." I shivered; this invisible menace became even more frightening.

The other end of the road was crowded with people and taxis. The university and some thirty villages were cut off from Ramallah, which was very inconvenient, but at least it brought the taxi drivers and street vendors some business. Dust flew into the air, people were shouting, and tempers were short. On his back, a vendor carried a brass samovar that was taller than a person, its spout curved some eight times. It was like a fantastic musical instrument. Then, with a heft of his shoulder and a twist of his waist, liquid poured out like music. He gave our leader, Russell, a free glass and then we all had a taste. It was like cold, sour plum juice and I felt much calmer.

We got out of the taxi and walked across the campus. It was no different from any other university campus around the world. Students chatted in small groups, enjoying the afternoon sunshine. The female students seemed quite open and none were wearing burkahs. Berzeit University is Palestine's first institution of higher education. When it was established in 1924, it was only a primary school, then gradually expanded until it became a full-fledged university in the 1970s. Over the past few years, fifteen students have been killed in demonstrations. The Israeli authorities routinely force the school to close down, and from 1979 to 1982 it was closed sixty-one percent of the time. Beginning in January of 1988, the school closed for fifteen consecutive months. During this time, the administration secretly organized temporary study groups off campus. Even so, it has taken many students ten years to finish the four-year program.

Unfortunately, no student representatives had been invited and the luncheon was somewhat flat. The president gave a welcome speech and Russell talked about the possibility of Berzeit University cooperating with a school in the U.S., perhaps with Princeton, where he taught. One professor told us that, because of the siege, many students slept in the classrooms at night.

I slipped out to wander around the building. Student sculptures were displayed in the main hall. One of them astounded me: a bird's egg placed in a nest of rusty iron nails. This form of imagination is heartbreaking, a mark of youth wounded by war.

We took a bus from the university to a refugee camp. These so-called refugee camps are actually temporary dwellings built for people expelled from their own homes; and they've been "temporary" for a number of generations. We first went to the refugee camp's recreation center. The door had been battered down by a tank, and the floor was strewn with bits of paper and broken glass. Computers, musical instruments, weight-lifting equipment—nothing had been spared. The person in charge of the center apologized, saying there wasn't a single good chair left for us to sit on. He spread open his hands and asked, "What do you think, is this a terrorist base?"

There were holes in almost every wall of each house. These were caused by an explosive weapon recently invented by the Israelis who were tired of the inconvenience of breaking down doors; now they can simply pass through walls. Perhaps this new technology will bring with it a new way of calling on people and change the traditions of human etiquette. We stopped at a refugee family's house deep in a small alley of the camp. When the "guests" came to call, they not only destroyed the television set, they also wounded their host. I don't understand Arabic, but the despair and hate in their gestures and expressions needed no translation.

At six in the evening the same day, Arafat wanted to see us. This wasn't written on the schedule, but no one seemed surprised by it. Leila, who was accompanying us, said Arafat could see us for only half an hour as he was supposed to meet with the Cabinet afterward. A police car led the way. It was just getting dark when we arrived at his official residence. The bus entered the main gate, drove through an empty area, and stopped at the gate of an ordinary-looking house where guards—guns loaded and ready to fire—stood at watch. We were brought to a lounge area where we all talked and joked quite casually, unaccustomed to the pressures of such a formal occasion. After about ten minutes, we were ushered to another room across the hall. Arafat was standing at the door, and after Leila's introductions, he shook hands with each member of the delegation. Arafat was wearing his famous smile. He looked no different from his photographs, but he was shorter than I had imagined. Short people have their own way of dealing with the world: in general they are more confident and stubborn, more pragmatic, and have a more combative spirit. The strategists and psychological experts in Israel have probably not considered these points.

The room was clearly both Arafat's office and reception room—at one end was a desk, and beside it stood a Palestinian flag; at the other end was a sofa, and a tea table with a delicate water lily on top. Arafat and our leader, Russell, sat in the middle. According to prior arrangements, this was not to be an open meeting, so all the reporters were chased out. Russell first said a few words on behalf of the International Parliament of Writers and expressed support for Palestine's independence and freedom. He especially emphasized our desire to see Darwish. Arafat pointed at Darwish and joked, "He's the boss." Each delegate said a few words, translated by Leila, and Arafat often answered in English. Soyinka said he hoped they would not write hatred and conflict into their textbooks. Arafat made a decisive gesture and said, "Absolutely not. We are doing quite the opposite, not paying nearly enough attention to historical description." He sighed and said that when he was a child, his home was near the Wailing Wall and he used to play with Jewish children all day. Now, this is impossible. I was the last to speak. I told him he has been a hero of mine ever since I was a child. And I wondered if he still held on to his early ideals after so many years and difficulties?

Arafat jumped up excitedly and pointed to the large photograph of the Temple Mount behind him—particularly the striking gold leaf Dome of the Rock and the Jewish temple beside it. The Temple Mount is a holy place, not just of Islam, but also of Catholicism and Judaism. It is where Jesus preached and the first altar of Abraham was built. Arafat drew a large circle with his finger, suggesting peaceful coexistence was his ideal. He used metaphor to observe and explain the world by alternative means. It was difficult to imagine his opponent, Sharon, using metaphor. Sharon's language was as blunt as a tank. And three days later, Sharon's tanks burst into Arafat's official residence.

The visit lasted about an hour, running over the allotted time, and the Cabinet meeting had to be postponed. Arafat posed for pictures with each of us. He also ran back and forth, fetching illustrated brochures of a Palestinian-Bethlehem development plan for the year 2000, along with souvenir badges that he gave to each of us. Breyten asked him to autograph his brochure. As we were about to leave, the mischievous Breyten crept up to Arafat's desk. One of the guards tried to stop him, but he managed to slip by and steal a piece of chocolate off the desk, putting it into his mouth.

At eight that night, at Ramallah's Al-Kasaba Theater, we gave a reading with a group of Palestinian poets. The house was packed. One person told me there hadn't been this kind of cultural event for a long time due to the siege. Darwish read first. From the sound of the appreciative sighs in the audience, one could sense he was the pride of Palestine. His poems made me think of the late Israeli poet Yehuda Amichai who I had met twelve years earlier at the International Poetry Festival in Jerusalem. There was, to my surprise, a certain similarity of tone in their poetry: the lonely quality of their words, their impotence and alienation regarding the state of things, their fear of the clamorous crowd, their attempt to maintain a last bit of dignity by mocking themselves. I don't know if they've read each other's work, and maybe this isn't important. What is important is that people of both cultures really listen to their poets. As Octavio Paz said, poetry is a third voice apart from religion and revolution. This voice cannot truly eliminate hatred, but perhaps can alleviate it to some degree.

For at least one night, poetry broke the siege of the language of hate.

Early the next morning, we were supposed to leave Ramallah and go to the Gaza Strip. I woke up early and turned on the television. The first item on the CNN six o'clock news was a shot of Arafat meeting us, followed by an announcement by a Palestinian spokesman that Arafat had decided not to attend the Arab summit meeting in Beirut. I didn't see the connection between these two stories, but this decision was obviously made at the Cabinet meeting. The superimposition of the two images gave me a feeling of having overstepped my station. Was his determination to struggle to the end strengthened by the support of the international writers?

Beginning the previous evening, two or three armed police had been stationed on each floor, standing watch with guns in hand. I heard Saramago's provocative remarks had roused the president of Portugal to personally call Arafat with the hope that he would guarantee his safety.

Darwish and the others came to the hotel to see us off. Tania gave me a tape of her concert in Paris and a book she had written. The last thing she said was, "Compared to Gaza, this place is paradise."

The road from Ramallah to Gaza is not long, but it took us almost three hours to get there, inching along in traffic. Before entering Gaza, we switched to a U.N. vehicle at the border inspection station, and a U.N. representative in charge of the aid office in Gaza joined us. Our luggage was removed and searched while we crossed the border. Then our passports were taken and we waited for more than an hour before an Israeli official finally returned to confirm our identities. Leila told me we were lucky because without the U.N.'s help, it would have been difficult to enter Gaza. And unless they have special approval, Palestinians can never leave.

We arrived in Gaza two hours behind schedule. As soon as

we passed the border, the car was surrounded by local jour-
nalists who had been impatiently waiting for us. But as time
was pressing, we couldn't give any interviews. Leila opened
the car door to explain this to them, but became angry and
the reporters had no choice but to stalk off. With her hands
on her hips, she told us, "They used to behave better and keep
their word, but now all they care about is American dollars,
and they'll beat their brains out to get one. Ugh!"

Then a middle-aged man walked over. His name was Raji
and he was the director of the Palestinian Centre for Human
Rights. Beads of sweat seeped across his balding forehead. His
English was fluent, but it had an obvious restlessness, his
words bouncing around like spent shells. Raji used to be a
lawyer, and was a human rights activist for many years. He
was once imprisoned by the Israelis. As the bus moved forward, he stood at the door and told us about the situation
in Gaza.

The Gaza Strip is a narrow belt of land that runs along
the Mediterranean Sea, forty-six kilometers long and six to
ten kilometers wide, all together about 360 square kilometers.
In Gaza, about 1,200,000 Palestinians occupy sixty percent of
the land, one of the most densely populated areas on Earth.
Israel controls forty percent of the land, including the settlements, the military base, and the buffer zone, yet there are
only some 6,000 Israeli immigrants, making up about half of
one percent of the total population. Three-fourths of the people of Gaza are refugees—driven from their homes by Israel in
1948—and their descendants.

The main highway in Gaza is controlled by Israel and is
reserved for the use of Israeli military and Israeli settlers.
Palestinians can only crowd onto a single unpaved road, and
even this road is disrupted by two checkpoints and closes at 5

p.m. Rush hour is simply a disaster, with a line of cars stretching into the distance from the guard posts. The road is narrow and accidents are frequent. There was an overturned truck by the side of the road right in front of us. Karen, the U.N. assistant representative in Gaza, was sitting next to me. She told me Israel was afraid of suicide bombers and made it a rule that every car had to have at least two people in it or it would not be allowed on the road. Even when she was driving a car with the U.N. logo, she tried to have her son ride with her as often as possible, just in case.

The car turned down a road along the coast. Blue sky, white waves, green trees—it was enough to take one's breath away. Raji told us that not long ago a delegation from Spain had visited and were shocked by the poverty of their Mediterranean neighbors. Israel holds maritime power and Palestinian fishermen can only fish within six kilometers of the coast. Passing by a field of strawberries, Raji said many of the strawberries Europeans eat are from Gaza, but they aren't aware of this because Gaza strawberries must first be shipped to Israel, where they are packaged and given an Israeli label before they are exported. Worse yet, even Gaza's groundwater is siphoned off by the Israelis, then sent back through pipelines and sold to the Palestinians in Gaza. Such blatant exploitation, with no need for concealment or obscurity, should be enough to make all the capitalists of the world sick with envy.

We drove into the neighborhood of an Israeli beach settlement. It was as if there had just been a battle. The road was pitted, most of the surrounding buildings were demolished, and the ruins were covered with the scars of gunfire. The settlement, circled by a high wall, had a blockhouse with guards. This was one of the nineteen settlements in Gaza. Raji told us that at this intersection alone, more than eighty people at a demonstration had died from Israeli gunfire, most of them young people.

Unlike the West Bank, Gaza is surrounded on all sides by Israel's barbed wire barricade. As I see it, aside from the economic extortions, the Israelis are content to let the Palestinians live or die as they will. Palestinians not only lack the freedom to come and go from Gaza, they are severely restricted from traveling within their own land. If Gaza is a large prison, then these settlements are small prisons, prisons within a prison, besieged on all sides by hatred. It is simply impossible for the Jewish settlers to have any contact with the locals as their comings and goings all depend on military escorts. I asked Karen, "Just what kind of person would be willing to move here?" She pointed to her skull. "What?" I said confused, "Is it a mental problem?" Karen laughed and replied, "No, people are just duped by advertisements—the beautiful landscape, low-priced housing. Most of the recent immigrants are old Jewish people from the States."

I asked Breyten if the situation here was in any way comparable to the old apartheid system in South Africa. He sighed and said he didn't think anybody could top the efficiency of Israeli officials. It's as though it has all been carefully orchestrated with computers: how to squeeze out the maximum, how to impose the greatest difficulty on these people's lives.

We continued on to the province of Rafah which neighbors Egypt at the end of Gaza. Before getting out of the bus, Leila warned us that this is an extremely dangerous area, Israeli soldiers might shoot at any time so everybody should stay together and not wander off. With children pressing against us, we followed a wretched street that ended at a great tract of ruins heaped with rubble—brick and tile, shards of glass. The border wall was just fifty meters away; Israel's blockhouses and tanks stared menacingly.

Raji told us that in order to establish a buffer zone at the border, Israeli troops had destroyed almost four hundred refugee homes in this area. On January tenth of this year alone, fifty-nine houses were torn down, and two days later forty more were demolished. Seventeen hundred refugees had no homes to return to. At best, the troops gave forty minutes for the refugees to gather some of their things; at worst they weren't given any notice.

A path opened in the crowd and a middle-aged woman (who looked much older) walked towards us. Through Leila's translation, she related the terrible events of that day. At two in the morning, with no warning, Israeli bulldozers roared in as adults shouted and children wailed. Scrambling and crawling, she managed to save her thirteen children, but all of their belongings were buried in the rubble. Then an old man who had heard that Russell was an American, shouted hoarsely, "Why do you Americans give airplanes and tanks to Israel? Who is the terrorist? Sharon is the real terrorist!"

My rage left me utterly spent, and I wandered around on my own. On the street I ran into Soyinka and Juan and we walked silently together. Not far ahead, a loudspeaker broadcasted music and slogans. On a banner at the mouth of an alley was someone's photo. We guessed it must be a new martyr. Shadowy figures swayed in a house where a feast was taking place; several elderly people were seated along the wall, smoking. It was full of cheer, like a funeral in our northern villages in China. A young man stopped us and invited us in. When he realized that we didn't understood Arabic, he called someone over who greeted us with a friendly, "Welcome!" Soyinka, though, pointed at his watch, saying, "Thank you very much, but we have to leave right away." They were a little let down.

When we got back to the car, Leila shouted, "I have been looking everywhere for you! We have to make it to the checkpoint before four-thirty, otherwise we won't be able to get through." A child of six or seven pulled on my hand, wanting me to take his photo. He squatted beside the vehicle making a "V" sign.

Our road led past the Rafah provincial highway police station where we stopped briefly. This place was quite close to the U.N. offices, and not long before had been blown apart by a missile from an Israeli helicopter. Hearing of our presence, the provincial governor rushed over. But we were pressed for time, and could only hurriedly shake hands and say our goodbyes.

We raced to the checkpoint, and even though U.N. vehicles drive in a special lane, there was still a line. The other lane was so packed with cars you could not see the end of the line. Raji wiped sweat from his forehead and said, "I have lived forty-eight years, and have never felt such despair. It is not poverty that people fear, but humiliation. Having to pass through a checkpoint every day is a form of humiliation."

Breyten pointed out the window at a young man who worked for Raji. His name was Li Zhiyi, an American-born Chinese whose parents lived in Taiwan. He couldn't speak much Chinese anymore. He was a tall young man, handsome and intelligent. While he was studying sociology at Harvard, he did volunteer work in India, and last year, after graduation, he came here to do an internship, planning only to stay three months, but had extended his stay once, then once again, and now planned to spend the summer here before returning to Harvard to work on his Master's degree. He said

his parents were both in hi-tech fields and didn't really understand him, and were also very worried. I agreed to give his
parents a call when I got back to the States to put their minds
at ease. While he spoke with me, he also chatted and joked
with some young Palestinians. His Arabic seemed fluent. I felt
proud of him. Not many overseas Chinese kids can separate
themselves from mainstream culture and go beyond the
boundaries of a materialistic life.

When the topic of suicide bombings came up, he said:
"The May 10th incident was entirely the work of people living
on the West Bank because people in Gaza have no way to get
out. It's also very difficult to get close to the settlements. Of
course there are those who risk their lives." He knew a young
Palestinian who ended his life this way shortly after getting
married.

We arrived at a hotel by the sea. Breyten and I were flying
out the next day, so we still had to hurry to Tel Aviv. Leila
arranged to have someone pick us up at 10:30. The other
members of the delegation were going to stay for two more
days to meet with local poets and anti-war groups.

Breyten and I were both tired but agreed to meet at the
hotel bar downstairs for a drink. The bar was deserted. We
asked a waiter and he said they were not selling any liquor because of the Intifada. I didn't understand. Breyten told me
this word referred specifically to the Palestinian resistance
movement. Stymied, we went and knocked on Russell's door.
He still had half a bottle of scotch. The window of his room
overlooked the Mediterranean Sea. The sky was dull and
cloudy, the water black and gray with layer after layer of white
waves curling up onto the shore.

Twenty minutes later, we all met downstairs and walked to
the offices of the Palestine Centre for Human Rights to hold

a press conference. Saramago was again the focus of the interview. In French, he said that some people dislike it when he uses this or that kind of word, but regardless, we must admit that Israel's actions are a crime against humanity.

A press conference with Palestinian writers in Gaza followed. Perhaps as a result of the scotch he had drunk, Russell was not his usual thoughtful, cautious self, and said, with some emotion, "I have spent most of my life being in the wrong place at the wrong time, but this time I have chosen the right place and the right time. . . ."

The Palestinian writers spoke marvelously. A young local writer said he had just received one of Saramago's novels from a friend and was reading it. He lived far away and wouldn't be able to return home this evening as the roads would be closed. He gave his Arabic version of the book to Saramago.

At 8 P.M., a reception was held in an elegant, old Arabic hotel. The vaulted main hall was encircled by a corridor, and candlelight flickered everywhere. I weaved between the pillars and ran into Madeleine Mukamabano from the French Culture radio station. Her entire family had died in the ethnic strife in Rwanda. When the International Parliament of Writers met in Lisbon in 1994, she, as an eyewitness, described the terrifying slaughter. When she talked about her impressions of Gaza, she said she felt it was more awful than what had happened in Rwanda. Compared with the mass slaughters, she added, this was a daily torment of both the body and spirit—more helpless, more painful.

Departure time came quickly, and we looked everywhere for Breyten. Someone said they had seen him upstairs. I looked everywhere, but there was no trace of him. I returned to the hotel to get my bags. A U.N. jeep was already waiting for us at the hotel gate. I asked the young Finn driving the jeep to wait, and I returned again to look for Breyten. He finally appeared, a little unsteady. I asked him if he had been drinking. He held his index finger to his lips: "Shhh. Intifada."

We had to stop at the Israeli inspection station at the Gaza border crossing. A soldier instructed the driver to park the car in a cement stall. A young woman soldier flirted with two male soldiers. We hauled our luggage into a room. A man in glasses was friendly, but that didn't get in the way of his carrying out his duties as he searched us from top to bottom.

The moon was bright and few stars were visible. There were almost no cars on the highway. I slept the whole way and when we got to the hotel in Tel Aviv, it was already half past midnight. Yael Lotan was waiting for us at the desk. She was about forty, Jewish, ran a small publishing house, and had volunteered to arrange some activities on this side of the border for the International Parliament of Writers. Breyten and I had to get up at five thirty the next morning and Yael insisted on going with us to the airport. I invited both of them to have a drink. First we went to the hotel bar, but the jazz band performing there was too loud, so we went to my room and phoned down for a bottle of red wine. Yael told us that Saramago's speech had made some big waves. He's very popular in Israel with one novel having sold more than 60,000 copies— a best-seller in Israel.

I asked Yael what she thought about the suicide bombings. She shrugged her shoulders and the lenses of her glasses flashed in the lamplight. "I like red wine. I like books." She paused, and said, "If I get blown up one day, I will have deserved it." She was willing to pay the ultimate consequence of the choices her people have made.

I only got a couple hours of sleep, crawled out of bed, and met Breyten in the lobby. Yael sauntered in late, which drove Breyten into a frenzy of impatience. We were fortunate to have her with us, though, because she greeted the airport security staff in Hebrew, after which they became considerably more polite to us. An ill-favored girl questioned me. Because my passport had been stamped, I couldn't deny that I had been to Ramallah and Gaza. Whether blunt or oblique, her questions, though complex, came down to simple matters: Who are you? Where are you coming from? Where are you going? I felt foolish because these are the very questions that I, myself, have trouble figuring out. Afterward, Breyten and I compared notes. Fortunately he had not said anything about Arafat, otherwise we really would have been in trouble.

The earth moved under our feet. We were soon on a British Air flight to London. I opened the local English newspaper, *The Jerusalem Post*, where there was a report on Arafat's meeting with us and the open letter from the Israeli ambassador to Portugal about Saramago. In it he said, "You chose to use a metaphor that we cannot accept, and what is even more difficult for us to accept is that a person who knows the power of words . . ."

Twenty-four hours later, Israeli forces mounted a large-scale attack on the West Bank and surrounded Arafat's official residence.

EMPTY MOUNTAIN

I

IN GERMANY ONE SUMMER, I stayed at a castle named Solitude, near Stuttgart. I was on a reading tour—from Munich to Berlin—with my German translator, Wolfgang Kubin. On the road back from Munich, we stopped to visit his younger brother in Dinkelsbuhl, a small and ancient town. The dates on the houses traced back to the Middle Ages. His brother's family lived on the edge of town. Wild ducks squawked on a nearby pond, furiously flapping their wings as if struggling to escape from the viscous stillness. Kubin's brother worked as an anesthesiologist in a hospital. From morning to night, he raced between painless stupor and sober wakefulness. His wife represented the wakeful world: home.

Kubin is one of those people who are strangers to fatigue. As soon as we had put down our luggage, he pulled me out to go for a walk. But this was no walk—it was nothing less than a forced march and I had to struggle to keep up. Every time I go out the door with him now, I feel some apprehension.

Weeds on the city walls rustled in the breeze; the walls were woven together with wooden ladders and stone passages. All I could hear was my own bellows-like panting and the pounding of my heart. Kubin spoke little, moving forward with great strides, frowning. He insisted on taking me to the place where a medieval executioner used to live. In those days, almost every town supported a professional executioner. We climbed up and down, turned corners, and searched for more than an hour. My legs had turned soft, and I was ready to plead for my own life before we even got to the executioner's house.

I met Kubin in 1981, at the Friendship Hotel in Beijing. Bonnie McDougall had invited us over for dinner, and her husband poured us glasses of Jinmen gaoliang (a sorghum liquor), which they had brought over from Hong Kong. Kubin was leaving Beijing the next day. I don't clearly remember my first impression of him. I do recall he had an interesting smile, like someone exhausted but resigned to laughing at himself in front of a mirror. In the spring of 1982, we saw each other in Beijing again, at the Summer Palace. I remember I hadn't slept well the night before, had forgotten to shave, and my whole body felt uncomfortable, like a potato freshly dug from the ground. Kubin produced a miniature German camera and aimed it at me. Neither of us liked to talk much. He was preoccupied that day, his eyes narrow, most likely due to the light reflecting off the lake. Kubin is three years older than me, but we were both young then.

Around that time, Kubin had recently finished his professorial qualifying thesis, *Empty Mountain*. His university studies touched on a wide range of subjects, including philosophy, Germanic studies, and sinology, but his major was divinity, and according to the original logical progression of things, he should have gone on to become Pastor Kubin. I recently read a Chinese translation of *Empty Mountain* re-titled, *The Chinese Literati's View of Nature*. In the preface to this book, the hitherto laconic Kubin finally dropped a clue: At the end of 1967,

Li Po's poem, "On Yellow-Crane Tower, Farewell to Meng Hao-Jan Who's Leaving for Yang-chou," convinced him to bid farewell to Protestantism and the Gospels. If a person changes his entire life because of a poem, it must be because of a mysterious calling rooted in the blood of his core.

Kubin was born in the northern German town of Celle. His ancestors were farmers for generations. His father was from Berlin and his mother was from Vienna. After his parents met, they moved to his father's mother's home in Celle. Although both belonged to the Germanic race, the Viennese are more moody and sentimental, producing great poets like Trakl and Rilke could arise. In the summer of 1985, I went with Kubin from Berlin to Vienna. Tracing his genealogy, the trip began at his father's house and ended at his mother's.

The rigidity of Berlin and the leisure of Vienna form a perfect contrast. In Vienna, we took the tram, clanging through neighborhoods during afternoon siesta. We went for a walk in the Vienna Woods, stopping at the spot where Freud told his friend, "Dreams explain everything." In the evening we drank young wine in a pub on the outskirts of town that Beethoven had frequented. In Vienna, even the Strauss waltzes performed by the street musicians are transformed, infused with a particular sorrow.

What Kubin enjoyed most was taking me to cemeteries. Soon after we arrived in Vienna, we paid calls on masters such as Beethoven, Mozart, and Schubert, listening carefully to the music of silence. The cemetery is a culture unto itself, a meeting place of history, religion, architecture, and language. Each gravestone can speak; the main character is dead, but the story is not over. When Kubin entered a cemetery, the lines on his face would soften, the natural rhythm of his stride change, now faster, now slower, vacillating among the graves.

Frowning, he'd read the inscriptions on the stones, then turn his head and walk away. I learned quite a few things from him at cemeteries, most importantly how to experience the silence of death.

To this day I still cannot understand how that simple poem by Li Po could have caused him to go down a completely different road:

> From Yellow-Crane Tower, my old friend leaves the west.
> Downstream to Yang-chou, late spring a haze of blossoms,
>
> distant glints of lone sail vanish into emerald-green air:
> nothing left but a river flowing on the borders of heaven.

2

SUIZI WARNED ME: "You had better not make Kubin sound so depressed in your essay. Some people look happy on the surface, but the moment you turn your head, they commit suicide. Our Kubin looks depressed, but it's no problem. . . ." I gave her my word. Suizi, Kubin's wife, used to work in the Beijing Library. Kubin was in Beijing researching supplementary material after having finished the first draft of *Empty Mountain*, and Suizi and another librarian sometimes helped him with his research. After a few visits they were no longer strangers, and one day this quasi-minister, who had never cast a stray look in his life, rushed to Suizi's office holding two tickets to a performance of *The True Story of Ah Q* in his pocket. But he got rattled, and when he got there, he didn't bring up the tickets and ended up going on a date with Ah Q. The chemical reactions between people are truly amazing, a kind of acid and base that neutralize each other. Suizi has many things to say, which fill the valleys left by Kubin's silence. No, Kubin corrects me, Suizi has many dreams.

Kubin often visited Beijing. Riding his battered bicycle he would fly all over the city. He said he had a lover in the library, and that it was not a book. At that time, marrying a foreigner was still a bit difficult, and his dates with Suizi were like guerilla attacks, coming without warning or regularity, adding another layer to their romance.

Besides being unreliable, memory is also arbitrary. For example, why are some details singled out while others are cast aside? And for the people involved in an event, to what degree could their various memories be reconciled? After Gu Cheng died, Kubin wrote a piece called "Fragment": "The first time I met Gu Cheng was in November 1984. One evening, Bei Dao met me under the flag in Tiananmen Square. It had gotten dark early, we rode our bicycles for a while and arrived at his place. Several people were stuffing dumplings. Bei Dao's wife, the painter Shao Fei, I remember clearly. Gu Cheng was also there, but I am not certain who the other person was, perhaps it was Xie Ye? Bei Dao began to help in the kitchen. Gu Cheng and I sat on the sofa and began our first conversation. . . ."

I am still surprised by the power of Kubin's memory. He was like a shaman who can supernaturally summon a mass of details from a deep night long ago. We were living west of Chongwen Gate, on Xi Damochang Street, very close to Tiananmen. Why did we choose to meet under the flag? Most likely because it was the most obvious landmark in Beijing. It got dark early that day, and the air was icy. With a drinker's sharp eye, I noticed the half dozen bottles of Danish Carlsberg beer (no doubt bought at the Friendship Store) in the plastic bag hanging from the handle of his bicycle. Taking advantage of the remaining daylight, I hurriedly led him through the five courtyards that led to my house, the air filled with the mildewy smell of cabbages that had been stored away for the winter. We propped our bicycles by the door. I pushed the door open and bright light poured out. Our house didn't have a sofa, so Kubin and Gu Cheng sat facing each other on two cushioned armchairs upholstered in red cloth. At first Gu Cheng was like a timid animal, nervous and afraid, but Kubin's fluent Chinese put him at ease, and he began to speak about the Cultural Revolution, about Fabre's *Souvenirs Entomologiques*—a fluid torrent of words, unstoppable once begun. And Xie Ye was indeed there that night, stuffing dumplings while looking approvingly at Gu Cheng. In addition to the Danish beer, Kubin and I also drank several glasses of Hengshui spirits. . . .

I drifted around Europe after 1989, often stopping in Bonn to see Kubin, and he always welcomed me with some hard liquor. Kubin made a kind of spicy, steaming hot tofu soup. We would sit across from each other without speaking and drink a string of shots "down in one." The good-hearted Suizi always worried that, one day, my exile ended, I would return home and be unable to find work. She suggested that I learn to drive so I could become a taxi driver, or perfect my English and become a tour guide.

Kubin and Suizi edited a German magazine called *Pocket Sinology*, and their lives were turned upside down by their work. Furthermore, the university's library funds were limited, and they had to dig into their own pockets to buy books and subscribe to periodicals. The space in their house shrank as the number of books grew, swallowing everything like a flood, surging into the hallways. I slept among the piles of books, dreaming with them, bumping into them until my back was sore and my legs ached.

Kubin was a genuine ascetic even though he had a wife and drank. What I mean is that he was extremely demanding of himself. No matter what hour he went to bed, at six o'clock the next morning he would sit at his desk to write and prepare classes. He would see me to the train station and carry my luggage, panting and puffing from the exertion, yet he never called a cab. I finally learned the meaning of the saying, "After the bitter comes the sweet," when, at the end of a long-distance trek, we sat in a bar at the edge of the Rhine drinking beer. Happiest of moments!

Later he quit drinking everything but milk in order to have more strength for writing his great work and for keeping his family fed. With his first wife he'd had a daughter who was now in college. Suizi gave birth to two boys, who were always crying to be fed. The place that they rented for years was taken over by books, and there was nothing to do but fall into the capitalist trap: buy a house on the installment plan. A professor's salary is uncomfortably tight. Unfortunately, when I went to his new house, I had to drink alone which was completely unenjoyable. I would drink until I could not see clearly, and then I'd stare at Kubin pounding away at the computer. Eventually resigned to the situation, I would sigh, tumble into bed, and fall asleep.

3

THE SUBTITLE OF THE ORIGINAL German version of *Empty Mountain* was "The Development of the View of Nature in Chinese Culture." Kubin believed that as early as the Wei-Jin period, that is, about fifteen hundred years ago, Chinese literature achieved a perfectly developed view of nature. People saw a landscape as an independent object, and thus sought to grasp its beauty. He divided the development of the Chinese view of nature into three stages, closely related to the growth of the aristocracy. He drew on a wide range of sources, and his views were extremely insightful. What surprised me was that a foreigner could organize the Chinese cultural tradition in such an orderly manner. The book's title, *Empty Mountain*, comes from Wang Wei's quatrain "Deer Park":

> No one seen. In empty mountains,
> hints of drifting voice, no more.
>
> Entering these deep woods, late sun-
> light ablaze on green moss, rising.

While talking with me about *Empty Mountain*, the philosopher Liu Xiaofeng once praised the work highly. Kubin and Liu are friends: one went from the West to the East, the other from East to West. They simply took different roads to the same goal, as one must distance himself from his own traditions in order to gain critical distance.

In November 1997, I went to Paris for a poetry festival, and made a detour to Bonn University to give a reading. Kubin took me for a walk in a cemetery on the slopes of a nearby mountain. The sky was heavy with clouds, full of rain yet to fall. The narrow paths through the cemetery were damp, meandering forward, leading us along, two lost living souls. Social class in the cemetery was clearly demarcated, and the attitudes to death were completely different: the rich flaunted their wealth in death, building resplendent graves for themselves, while the graves of the poor writers and artists were simple and dignified.

Our talk continued off and on. Kubin showed me the graves of philosophers, expressionist painters, and ministers killed by the Nazis. I asked Kubin about his beliefs. He stared for a long time at his large leather shoes as they swung forward one after the other, raised his head, and looked at the charcoal pencil-sketch branches of the trees. Slowly and hesitantly he said he'd probably still consider himself a Protestant. Every Sunday he went to the chapel at Bonn University and listened to the lectures of the professors in the divinity department. Liu Xiaofeng says he is a follower of Christ, but not a Christian. I think that the same is true for Kubin. Religious belief is related to the pain in one's heart, and places little emphasis on exterior form. But my real question for him was: Had he really returned to the path he had strayed from, or was he still fleeing towards the empty mountain in the East? I didn't ask. Some things are better left unsaid.

Kubin is a poet, and poets have the right not to explain their work. I read his early poetry—simple, brief, measured, and rich in philosophical ideas. A collection of his poems was set to be published at the end of that year. He has written three poems for me, but he cannot find the right person to translate them, so they remain within a German night I cannot penetrate.

Last spring, while teaching at a college in the Midwest, Kubin and his family visited me in California. Their two sons got along well with my daughter, running madly up and down the stairs with her. Suizi was no longer urging me to become a taxi driver or a tour guide. Now, with no trace of a job in sight, it was almost time for me to think about retiring. She was still anxious about my future, asking about this and that, looking here and there to see if she could find any cracks in my life.

I nevertheless went along with Suizi's kind wishes for me and became a taxi driver and tour guide for them, taking the whole family to San Francisco. Kubin had bought a German travel guide beforehand, and not only had he read it carefully, he also firmly believed in the book's authority—"Look, San Francisco has three stars. We should go there." He also found it impossible to pass any sign in a museum, botanical garden, or on the side of the road without reading it from beginning to end.

I eventually realized that ever since I had known Kubin, the time we spent together was not linear—years and personal matters, media and solitude, friendship and violence were all woven together. It was closer to an Eastern form of cyclic time. The result was a kind of illusion of us always sitting together, silent in the presence of what has passed and what had yet to pass.

On the last night at his brother's house, Kubin brought me to the town center of Dinkelsbuhl. Every evening at nine thirty, a night watchman dressed in a traditional costume and carrying a spear with a cow's horn under his arm, sets out from the church and leads a mighty band of spectators to all the inns and taverns. This ancient tradition is now a tourist attraction. The watchman first blows his horn, then raises his voice and sings an age-old melody, but the words are always improvised. At the sound of his horn, waiters come out bearing a glass of wine, first tasted by the watchman and then shared with the crowd. As we were waiting for the watchman to appear, Kubin and I sat on a stone bench by the church, silently watching the flickering lights of the town. Save for the headlights of cars, this sight has not changed much for centuries. People come and go, disappear, including us so-called spectators.

I had forgotten the town's name and phoned Kubin. The next day he sent a fax. Aside from "Dinkelsbuhl," only the first character of his Chinese name was written. The piece of paper was an empty mountain with him at its center.

POUL BORUM

EVERY TIME I HAVE TO look for someone's business card and flip through, one by one, all the names in my dark blue plastic box, I get a headache. As I glance at the names, I realize that the people I don't remember and the people I dislike far outnumber the rest. Looking for a business card is a bit like going to a raucous gathering: people recognize one another, call out, respond, avoid, and plot against each other. . . . Of course, if it is absolutely necessary, you can tear up those you dislike and toss them in the garbage—and not just in theory. You will also find some dead among them, which is normal, as sooner or later we all have to retire from behind our names. Whenever I used to look for a business card, Poul Borum would elbow his way out of the crowd to greet me. His business card was simple and unadorned—a Copenhagen address and telephone number printed under a pale blue name.

Beginning in the fall of 1990, I taught for two years at the University of Aarhus in Denmark. Though Aarhus is the second largest city in Denmark, it is not much bigger than a county seat in China. The sea there was permanently gray, like my mood.

The Danish translation of my collection of poems, *Old*

Snow, was published in the fall of 1991. As I walked home from class one day, I bumped into my landlord, Olaf, who was divorced and a retired architect. He said there was a review of my new collection of poems in the newspaper, and invited me to his place to sit for a while before dinner. Olaf lived on the first floor. His living room was spacious and bright, the panes of the half-opened window reflected the reddish gold trees, and a Sony pocket transistor radio was broadcasting Beethoven's Pastoral Symphony. He poured us two glasses of Spanish wine, got out the newspaper, and translated the review into English, sentence by sentence. He overestimated the level of my English. I listened without really understanding anything except that it was generally positive, which I deduced from Olaf's facial expressions. He was proud to have me as his tenant, someone who both made it into the newspaper and paid his rent on time.

The next day, my boss and Danish interpreter, Anne, told me that the reviewer was Poul Borum, a central figure in Danish poetry. In addition to his own poetry and translations, he also wrote criticism and scripts for television movies, as well as a newspaper column where he thoroughly appraised Danish and all northern European poetry. His language was cutting and he used poetry to demarcate boundaries—the majority of poets he reviewed were driven out by his column, commonly referred to as "Borum's Court." Anne also reminded me that the *Anthology of Contemporary Northern European Poetry* I had helped translate into Chinese in the mid-eighties included one of Borum's poems as well as six poems by his ex-wife, Inger Christensen. Unfortunately, I had brought nothing with me but the Chinese language.

Two weeks later, Anne passed on Borum's greetings to me, along with his telephone number in Copenhagen. I trembled as I dialed, as if I were phoning God. "This is Borum," he said in a gentle, slightly hoarse voice. His English was fluent, making me even more tongue-tied. This linguistic inequality was bound to make for serious psychological obstacles. Fortunately, his attitude seemed sincere and friendly, otherwise we probably would never have met face to face.

Unlike Aarhus, Copenhagen is an international city, and on this leg of my exile, the last stop on my flight from reality. At that time, there were problems with both my passport and my visa, and I could not leave Denmark. Previously when I was in Copenhagen, I boarded the wrong train and nodded off, "not knowing I was just a guest in my own dream," and almost accidentally crossed the border into Germany. The conductor was fortunately checking tickets and woke me up. Otherwise, I would certainly have been stuck in the middle of some bureaucratic machinery.

Mr. Borum's appearance startled me. He was bald with a square jaw and enormous ears, a large earring dangling from his left ear. Dressed in a black leather jacket with a fringe and metal snaps, he wore a broad belt around his waist and steel-toed boots. A complete underworld godfather. Where did this outfit come from? I knew quite a few former hippies who now dressed respectably. He had apparently refused to change his costume after the set changed.

Borum's large apartment was on the third floor of an old building, and it was as complex as a labyrinth. At five p.m. it was already dark in Copenhagen. Light from several lamps revealed partial details in the darkness: a fax machine, papers, a record player, some folders. The dim lamplight led us toward an open space. I had never seen such a large private library: bookshelves filled the length and breadth of the room. Borum said he had more than fifty thousand volumes in his collection, mostly poetry, each book entered in a computer in alphabetical order. He quickly found several volumes of my poetry in Swedish and Danish on the meticulously arranged shelves. With a few words, Borum sent away a hireling who helped keep the books organized.

We sat in the dim light. Borum's talk ranged far and wide, and he busied himself with one thing or another, but I could feel him observing me. He looked at his watch, said he had reserved a table at a restaurant, then called a taxi. I walked with him through a series of rooms. He opened the back door, locked it, and we stepped into a narrow, old-fashioned elevator that looked like it descended to hell. The elevator was sluggish and creaky, and we were crowded together like twin embryos in a mother's womb. The light of a small lamp shined on Borum's bald head, and his expression was strange. The elevator finally stopped. There was no hell. The air outside was cold and fresh.

At a French restaurant downtown, I ordered a bottle of port, pretending to be an expert. The waiter clearly knew Borum and was extremely deferential to him, even lighting his fat cigar. Borum started puffing away like a steam engine, smoke weaving between our words. He admitted that he didn't understand many of my poems, but he liked them. When we started talking about our mutual friend, Allen Ginsberg, I learned that Borum had lived in the U.S. for many years and had been a part of the Beat Generation. With two glasses of wine in my stomach, "Mr. Borum" became "Poul." On closer inspection, there was a kind of benevolence in his features, but he also had an aura of authority, like an abbot in a Buddhist temple, that didn't fit with the bad-boy reputation he had all over northern Europe. In truth, everybody lives in the midst of misunderstanding, but some people

don't care about being misunderstood. He drank very carefully, taking only a tiny sip each time he drank. I, on the other
hand, drank too quickly, and as some of my friends have
noted, my eagerness for drinking is greater than my tolerance.
I ordered another bottle. Gradually, I started to shake, then
there was a wave of dizziness, and Poul's voice disappeared in
the cigar smoke.

When I opened my eyes, Poul was looking at me with
concern.

"Are you all right?"

"What? Did I fall asleep?"

"You slept for more than half an hour."

"I'm sorry."

"No problem. You were tired."

I couldn't believe I had actually fallen asleep at the dinner
table across from my host in a foreign country. I rubbed my
forehead and refilled my glass. On the way home, I fell asleep
again in the cab.

The next time I saw Borum it was already winter. We sat in
a small coffee shop next to the central square of Copenhagen,
looking out the window at the blowing snow. He had also invited Inger Christensen and another female poet. Poul as-
sured me that Inger was the best poet in Denmark. I was willing to believe him. One look at Inger and you could see she
was one of those remarkably intelligent women from another
era. She had an innate wariness of masculine incorrigibility.
But we did not get along. Poul and Inger were still good
friends. They exchanged glances from time to time in a silent
understanding that is only possible from many years of
shared life. I had learned my lesson and was drinking more
temperately. I ordered a single beer.

"In this computer age," I announced, "books will soon

disappear." No one was shocked. Inger's lip curled, and she mumbled a few phrases to the effect that such alarmist talk didn't mean much. Borum said nothing, but smiled generously from inside his cloud of smoke. Inger reminded me that when I spoke English I never differentiated "word" and "world" clearly. Rather argumentatively, I retorted that "word" and "world" were in fact the same thing.

Winter passed into spring, and I saw Poul less and less often. He wanted to arrange a time to meet Anne and me for a chat, probably to clarify the relationship between "word" and "world," but unfortunately we never found a time that worked for everyone. By the fall of 1992, after I'd moved to the Netherlands, I had lost touch with Poul. Later, Anne told me he had been diagnosed with cancer. I tried calling him several times, and then gave up. What could I say? That "word" and "world" were definitely not the same thing?

In the spring of 1996, I received a letter from Anne saying Poul had just died, and that his friends had celebrated his sixty-fifth birthday party without him. I tried to find Poul's business card—the final connection between us. Weaving through the boisterous crowd, there wasn't even a shadow. He had gone away, without a greeting, without a goodbye.

BREYTEN BREYTENBACH

It's dark outside. Against the slanted window set into the roof there is this very soft rustling of rain coming down. I can look at it and I can see the wet tracks on the dusty surface. Across a dark space beyond the building there are windows alight and if one looks long enough you can see people moving behind the curtains, intent upon their nightly tasks and fancies, each living in his own little cocoon of fantasy and desire and ritual and habit.

—Breyten Breytenbach,
from *The True Confessions of an Albino Terrorist*

I

AUGUST 1975, JAN SMUTS AIRPORT, Johannesburg. A man called Galaska, who is holding a French passport, is apprehended while trying to board a flight back to Europe. Before his capture, he rushes into the restroom and swallows a slip of paper. He is taken to a room in the airport where a certain Colonel Snaaks of the South African Bureau for State Security has him write out his curriculum vitae. Relying on his writer's imagination, he compiles a life history and social network for Galaska. The colonel's aide then discovers a pipe while searching his bags. The captain has him hold the pipe in his hand, then bursts out in Afrikaans, "Come on Breyten, the game's up, we know who you are. Do you want us to go and fetch one of your brothers and confront you with him?" Breyten would later discover that at the same time this was happening to him, the Prime Minister of South Africa was returning from overseas travels, and a number of important figures and high-ranking officials were in the airport to welcome him back, including Breyten's older brother.

I have been rereading Breyten's *Confessions* recently. On the title page, he signed: "To my dear friend and singing partner Bei Dao, with best wishes, September 29, 1994, Lisbon." Besides his English name, he also used pinyin to spell out his Chinese name, Bian Tingbo.

In the fall of 1994, the International Parliament of Writers' executive committee held a meeting in Lisbon. One evening, we decided to go downtown to listen to some Fado. Even the price of sorrow is high for the restaurants and bars with Fado performances were shockingly expensive, and there were people at the doors whose sole job was to lure foreign tourists. Breyten took the lead, slipping away from the great throng of people while dragging behind me and his old friend Julianne. Breyten was a credit to his training in the underground. While chatting with a group of people, he signaled us with a glance to slip down an alley, and then followed us. We walked along a route Breyten had mapped out beforehand, stopping at a small bar frequented only by locals. Heavy smoke hung in the air, and the place was jam-packed. The singer was a young man, determined to wring out every bit of his pain through song. Fado reminded me of Shanxi opera— sad, shrill, sonorous, and viscerally stirring. We arrived too

late, and the show finished soon after we arrived. But our
spirits were still high and we stayed to drink. On our way
back to the hotel, under the influence of alcohol and Fado, we
began to hum softly in the dark night, each of us pouring out
our sorrow. Somehow the sad songs of these different countries blended into "L'Internationale." With Breyten singing in
English, Julianne in French, and I in Chinese, it was as harmo-
nious as if we had been practicing for a lifetime. In the middle
of the night, in the middle of Lisbon's bustling streets, we
strode along with our heads high, releasing our voices, singing this song that is in the process of being forgotten by the
world.

I can't remember exactly when I first met Breyten. We certainly ran into each other ten years ago at the Rotterdam
International Poetry Festival. I had just left China and could
not remember anybody that I met; people and dates were
shuffled together like a deck of cards. It must have been after
1989 that we were formally introduced. In Rotterdam in the
summer of 1990, Breyten suddenly popped up like the King of
Spades. He had the dignity of one who has suffered, his skin
was dark, his beard graying. What left the deepest impression
on me were his eyes, full of compassion, but with something
sharp in them that women especially needed to be wary of.
He had something of the clergy about him as well, though
he was definitely not your ordinary minister, and even less a
red-robed bishop. No, he was more like Christ himself—an
African Christ. I even called him Christ once and he just
looked at me blankly, "Me?" Then he chuckled and called
me "Mao."

Breyten was one of the policy makers for the Rotterdam
International Poetry Festival, and he attended almost every
year. He was a public figure, both the media and the other

conference attendees were always willing to lend him an attentive ear. He spoke trenchantly and never backed down when the truth was on his side. I have always been rather tongue-tied in such situations and, forced to speak in English as well, I become inarticulate and unable to get my point across. Born under the sign of the yellow croaker, I generally prefer to stay on the sidelines. I would occasionally run into Breyten when he was tired of the public, and we would spend time together talking, cracking jokes, and relaxing. Gradually, we became friends.

Confessions is the second volume of a three-book memoir. The first, *A Season in Paradise*, details Breyton's first trip home after being exiled for three years. That was in 1973, when he was given a three-month visa. In 1991, after Mandela regained his freedom, Breyten again returned to South Africa for three months and finished the third volume, *Return to Paradise*. Together, these three books can be viewed as an individual's chronicle of contemporary South Africa. I only own the *Confessions*. Reading it is like entering his life through an emergency exit, seeing both the future and the past from the position of his "now." Dante's *Divine Comedy* moves from inferno through purgatory and on to Heaven. *Confessions* is set in purgatory, definitely the bitterest days of Breyten's life.

Colonel Snaaks made his first appearance in *A Season in Paradise*, near the end of Breyten's trip home. One evening, his brother invited over two guests, one of whom was Colonel Snaaks. It was a warning calculated to let Breyten know beyond a shadow of a doubt that the government was aware of his covert activities. Two years later at the airport, the same Colonel Snaaks asked him to hold his pipe, saying: "The game's up . . ." Breyten was famous for smoking a pipe. After coming into South Africa under an assumed name, he switched to cigarettes. One day, walking through the Cape Town open-air market, he could not endure the tempting scent of cured tobacco, so he bought a pipe and some shredded tobacco and returned to his hotel for a secret smoke.

Breyten wrote: "Look how they dig into one's past, how they project one's future, how they alter one's present. I have no private lives: it's all in their hands; they know the I better than I do, they are far more interested in it than I am. They have the files, they have the computer. Or they know all about my ways, my preferences, my accretions, my little secrets—my gardens—be they political or sexual."

After spending more time with Breyten, I realized he was a natural born revolutionary, as sensitive as a harp string. And even though this harp string has been played cruelly by the wind, it has never broken, which is truly a miracle. And miracles arise from suffering, like the fate of Christ himself.

2

I LEFT THE U.S. FOR A POETRY festival in Durban. As I was changing planes in Johannesburg International Airport, the loudspeakers announced, "Mr. Breytenbach, please come to Gate 18 for boarding immediately, the plane is about to take off." Twenty-three years ago, Mr. Breytenbach was arrested a few minutes before he was to board a plane.

After arriving in Durban and setting my bags down at the hotel, I was led to an Italian restaurant. Breyten stood up and welcomed me, hugging me tightly and saying, "Hey mate! Welcome to South Africa." We had seen each other in Paris,

Mexico City, Lisbon, Strasbourg, Hong Kong and other places, but this time I was finally a guest in his home. Breyten would not agree with this statement, as he views the world as his home, living most of the time in Paris, summering in Spain, and then coming to South Africa for three months a year to teach writing at the university and to help organize the Poetry Africa Festival. I think South Africa occupies as much space in his mind as it does time in his calendar. He has no homeland; he belongs to an intermediate region of his own definition.

That night was the opening reception for an exhibition of his paintings. Unfortunately, I arrived two hours late and just missed it. Breyten the painter and Breyten the poet are two mirrors between which the real Breyten conceals himself.

I brought up the other Breytenbach whose name I overheard at the Johannesburg airport. He said that this name was not at all common in South Africa, and it was most likely one of his relatives.

The earliest Breytenbachs came to South Africa from Germany, and during their diverse migrations, Dutch, African, and Malay blood mixed, making their own bloodline as varied as an artist's palette. His grandfather was a farm laborer, but in his father's generation things were somewhat better. In accordance with the Chinese class system, he would have been considered a "middle peasant." With his own hands, he dug channels, plowed fields, and mined. Breyten has two older brothers and an older sister. His oldest brother was the one who welcomed the Prime Minister of South Africa when Breyten was arrested at the airport. He was a brigadier-general in the anti-guerilla special unit. The second oldest was a journalist who was sympathetic to fascism—a fellow-traveler with the secret police—and Breyten was a poetry-writing "terrorist." I was very curious about his relationship with his brothers. "It's okay," he said, "but when we're together we never talk politics." When he was living in exile in Paris, his eldest brother visited on business, and the two of them went from bar to bar, drinking until dawn.

In *Confessions*, Breyten pours out his thoughts to an omnipresent "Mr. Investigator," sometimes called "Mr. Eye," or "Mr. I." The tone of his language is full of sarcasm. As I see it, "Mr. Investigator" serves a dual role. He is both a co-conspirator with the secret police, and he is the only audience for the internal monologue of a man in despair. If Breyten is Christ, "Mr. Investigator" is God: "Ah, Mr. Investigator, don't you think I'm guilty? Yes, I have the guilt of the survivor."

Huntingdon, the chief of the secret police was a sick man. Once Breyten was summoned outside the gates of the prison where Huntingdon introduced him to his niece who was studying to be a teacher. She was a fan of his poetry and broke into tears at the thought of his suffering. On another occasion Huntingdon invited Breyten to his house and took him on a tour of the garden. Behind it was a mountain where there seemed to be no one on guard. Was this a hint that Breyten should run? Or a trap so that Huntingdon could shoot him down in flight? His two daughters asked Breyten to write something in their visitors' book. After lunch, the phone rang. Returning from the call, Huntingdon asked if Breyten wanted to take a shower and even offered him his toothbrush. But, Huntingdon was sorry to say, they would have to take him back, which he did, bringing him back to the prison office where Breyten's wife was waiting.

On the afternoon of my third day in Durban, Breyten and

his wife invited me to lunch at a Chinese restaurant. May in South Africa is already winter, but it was not at all cold. Like California in the summer, the sunlight was delightful. People were windsurfing on the ocean. The Chinese restaurant was right next to one of the big hotels. Breyten was sitting there waiting for me. He put down his newspaper, his gaze searching around him as if he wanted to know what my first impressions of South Africa were. I gave him a poem that I had just written: . . . *the madness you set free / is the silence-forging truth / as proud as the glistening of an internal injury / causes talk to grow dim . . . // wind in the rut of reading / salutes the pain beyond the blue silk. . . .*

Breyten asked if there were any developments in my China situation. I said the oracles were saying I could return next year. He stared at me, grinning. Facing this exile who had experienced all of his hardships, I felt a little green. He gave a poem to me in return that mentioned oracles and homesickness, and was full of affection.

Breyten's wife, Lien, was also there. She wasn't very tall, but she was elegant. We had never met face-to-face, only spoken on the telephone. Lien was Vietnamese of Chinese descent but couldn't speak Chinese. In South Africa, their marriage used to be illegal. Unlike in China, here it was not necessary for Lien's family to check out Breyten's class background for the previous three generations; but, as a white man, Breyten was not permitted to marry a woman of color. Lien had run all over the world advocating for him. A quarter of a century went by, and the shadow of Breyten's turbulent life had left its mark on her face—a pale melancholy. When Lien looked at Breyten, she had a look of both love and resignation, as if he were a troublesome child. Lien told me her full

name was Hoang Lien, and in Chinese it would be, Huang
Lian. I was startled, but didn't tell her the associations of her
name in Chinese.*

The owner of the restaurant was a bustling woman from
Shanghai. I ordered drunken chicken, steamed fish, and
home-style tofu, all of which were very authentic. Breyten
and I drank Tsingtao beer, while we talked. Whenever I visited
Paris, if Breyten was there, we'd go to a Cantonese restaurant
called Dajia Le in the Troisième Arrondissement. Those are
rare moments of leisure. Now it seemed like we were sitting in
the same place, only the scenery outside the window had
changed. He looked out at the children playing in the park by
the street and laughed out loud.

The trial began. Breyten wrote: "I can understand how the
mouse is paralyzed although still alive whilst being eaten by
the snake—celebrating with open eyes its own death." The oppressive courtroom, constructed with inlaid wood, was once a
synagogue. Day after day, the trial continued, witnesses coming and going, his father in the audience, staring silently. In
the end, Breyten was sentenced to nine years in prison.

Huntingdon brought him to the office. He seemed to be
both shocked and angered by the harsh sentence, but his sub-
ordinates entered one after another to congratulate Huntingdon. Someone even went so far as to take Breyten to the restroom and pour him a glass of wine, apparently so he could
celebrate this important day with them. Finally, Huntingdon

---

* Huang Lian ("Yellow Lotus") is associated with the saying, "a mute
eating yellow lotus," meaning, "to suffer in silence." So one who eats the
bitter yellow lotus and cannot speak, eats bitterness and is unable to
complain about it.

brought Breyten to his cell, where he sat across from him wearing dark glasses. Huntingdon spoke about the naiveté of his own youth, his difficult familial circumstances, and how he had climbed from being the president's bodyguard to his present position. As he related this story, his face became sickly white—as he felt a sort of orgasmic satisfaction. During the time Breyten was incarcerated, Huntingdon published all of the poems Breyten wrote on the condition that he dedicate the book to him.

3

READING BREYTEN'S MEMOIR IS NOT easy for me. His vocabulary is rich, and he mixes in French and Afrikaans. The book is like a wild river, and I am a narrow riverbed filled and then flooded by his words. But sometimes it's the opposite, I am no longer the so-called "passive reader" as I eagerly jump in and take part in the writing. I am Breyten in 1975, sentenced to nine years in prison. . . . I was followed the very minute I returned to my country. Actually, even earlier—when I applied for a visa in Rome with Galaska's passport, the net was already wide open. I shaved off my beard and sideburns, changed my hair, and wore broad-rimmed glasses. On the plane back to South Africa, I got to know a stewardess named Anna, and she gave me her phone number.

I passed through customs without a hitch. For the first few days, I roamed around and disappeared into the crowd. First I looked up friends who were not involved in politics, and then made contact with underground groups. After I was arrested, Huntingdon said they had even taken away every bottle of liquor that I had drunk before the cleaners got to my hotel room.

Anna called me at the hotel to arrange to see a play with me. Her marriage didn't seem to be working out; her husband had abandoned her. She showed me around a scenic spot near Johannesburg. When she flew out, I moved into her apartment.

I came to Cape Town and settled down on that quiet promontory, often meeting with underground groups. Once, after they had driven over to pick me up, we discovered that a white Ford was following us. We wove our way to the center of Cape Town, and I leaped out of the car and dove into the basement of a shopping center, took off my windbreaker, put on a wool hat, and rushed out through another exit. In the afternoon, I took the bus and slipped back to the hotel. I didn't turn on my light. Through my window I saw the white Ford, and in it two men smoking. There was a sudden storm, waves pounding against the cement piers. I spent the entire night destroying documents. Before dawn, I went out the back of the hotel, climbed over the courtyard wall, and boarded a bus. When I arrived at the last stop downtown, just after I got off the bus, the white Ford appeared at the intersection. I broke into a run, careening past the empty stalls of fruit sellers. It was like a scene from a third-rate action movie.

I somehow managed to throw them off and hid in an old friend's house. In the evening he drove me away, and I boarded a train in another town. When I returned to Johannesburg, I looked for Anna. She was just getting ready to go hiking in the mountains with some friends and I joined them. I had no idea that I had thrown myself into their trap—even Anna was one of the secret police. . . .

And I don't know why, but a Chinese poet became especially interested in this part of the story, and he replaced me, not only using the first person, but also compressing ten pages of narration into a few short paragraphs.

Breyten, because I believe escape is an eternal theme, not only you and I, but also everyone who does not identify with authority is also in flight. In May 1998, I strolled into the city hall of Durban, the largest port in South Africa, where Breyten's paintings were on exhibit. There were not many people inside. An old man shook his head with dissatisfaction at the paintings, mumbling to himself. Most of Breyten's paintings were self-portraits, full of irony directed at himself. He arbitrarily portrayed himself as a cow, or a horse, or Mao Zedong. Sometimes he had a fish, the symbol of Christ, on his head; other pictures were covered with male and female sex organs.

He once confessed to me that after he got out of jail, he was woman crazy. In Paris, he lived with a woman from southern Europe who even bore his child. The cords of feeling were like a net entrapping him. Lien accepted this fact and raised the child as her own daughter.

We are not saints and have no right to judge other people's indiscretions. The indelible memory of prison life is something those of us fortunate enough to be standing on the other side of its high walls cannot understand. When I first read *Confessions*, I woke up from nightmares, frightened and gasping for breath. Sometimes I had to skip over a section, like a needle skipping over an old record.

In South African prisons, newly sentenced inmates are all put in solitary confinement for a three-month "observation period," but Breyten's "observation period" was prolonged for almost two years. The devastation inflicted on a person by such absolute isolation is profound. Breyten talked to ants, played chess with himself, and was delirious with joy when a bird flew into the compound.

In the winter of 1982, Breyten was released and returned to Paris. I heard that every morning during his first year there, he would go to the Luxembourg Gardens near his home and run a few laps barefoot, crying as he ran. His mind was still following the routine of the prison: Every morning for half an hour, the prisoners were let out for some air.

Breyten used to be the treasurer of the International Parliament of Writers; in other words, he was in charge of its economic lifeline. The Parliament's core members included French thinkers such as Derrida and Bourdieu. Breyten detested empty literary theory. At the Lisbon meeting in the fall of 1994, in an interview for a French television station, he said, "We should liberate ourselves from the language of the French salons." He told me it was a minor television station and the interview aired on a morning program. There was no more than a hundred viewers, but to his surprise, Derrida had watched the interview and called him up to ask what exactly he had meant by that remark. Breyten shot right back: "I have the right to say this; that is, if you believe we still live in a free country."

Under pressure from the French government and PEN International, the South African authorities had no option but to grant Breyten an early release. The release came suddenly on December 2, 1982. Lien was planning to fly to Paris the same day, but before leaving, she prepared to see him one more time. On the morning of December 1, Breyten was taken to a room in a high-class downtown hotel where some important South African politico visited him. On the way back to the prison, as the drivers of the transport were passing by the sea, they slowed and let him roll down his window to breathe the salty air. Later that day he wrote a letter to Lien which he planned to give to her when they met the following day: ". . . I don't know whether that moment has arrived. . . . All these years you came closer to me, ever more precious. And I know you less now than I ever did. You are so strong it is a mystery to me. . . ." The next day, Lien was unable to visit him at the prison, and Breyten was sent out to work as usual. At noon he was brought to the prison office, then the warden announced his release. He didn't hear anything, he just stood in the doorway watching a white cloud on a mountain question the silence.

As far as I know, Breyten has never had an identity crisis. He can speak Afrikaans, English, French, Spanish, and Italian. Now he is a French citizen, and he also holds a Senegalese diplomatic passport. I asked him how he had managed this. He told me smugly that the president of Senegal was a buddy of his: "I can swagger back home whenever I please. Or . . . get posted to the Beijing consulate as a cultural attaché or something."

As *Confessions* drew to a close, I was mentally and physically exhausted; trying to keep up with Breyten's pace wasn't easy. I wanted to talk to him and phoned everywhere, but I couldn't find him. At that time of year, he should have been in South Africa. But how could one be sure? He flies all over the world, and these days he's on the road most of the time.

Take-off. High in air above land. More champagne offered discreetly. Compliments of personnel. Africa underneath, slipping away, my love. . . . So long. Not a word, no. . . . Lady One Hoang Lien's hand in mine. . . . We are to arrive at Roissy-Charles de Gaulle at 21:40. It will be raining. It is done . . .

THE MASTER OF ITHACA

GERMAIN DROOGENBROODT IS A Belgian poet. He worked
in the business world for many years, primarily reselling
cheap German cars at inflated prices in Taiwan, accelerating
modernization and increasing air pollution. Twelve years ago,
he sold his company and, near the Alexander Harbor, built
a manor in the small town of Altea, which overlooks the
Mediterranean. The manor is called Ithaca. Germain likens
himself to Odysseus—abroad for twenty years on business—
but it was not Belgium he returned to. He settled down in his
spiritual home of Spain.

There are many businessmen who style themselves
artists—they all have the same dream. But money is like
power, and you can't set it aside so easily. Germain was an exception. After twenty years of work, he bought his freedom.

In mid-May of 1989 there was a meeting of PEN International in Maastricht, Holland. The organization's chairman
asked me to say a few words about the Wei Jingsheng case. As
soon as I stepped onto the platform, Jin Jianfan from PEN
China left in protest along with two other members. A poet
from PEN Taiwan, Luo Qing, was my interpreter. Germain
was also there, a friend of Luo Qing. Who would have ex-

pected that this speech would twist together literature, politics, friendship, and also a certain Mr. Jin, who was himself a rope who tried to bend people into his visage until they grimaced. Not long after the Tiananmen incident, Jin Jianfan published an article in *Wenyi Bao* (*Literature and Arts Gazette*) titled "PEN International—Wei Jingsheng—Bei Dao." It was an extremely malicious attack.

After the conference, Germain drove Luo Qing and me to Bruges, Belgium. This ancient city is crisscrossed by canals and hooked together by stone bridges; many of the medieval buildings are in pristine condition. We sat beneath a sunshade, drinking Belgian beer, watching the tourists. Germain was an excellent conversationalist and asked many questions. He had evidently read quite a few books about China. His complexion was ruddy, his eyes bright, and on his chin grew a meticulously trimmed beard. In the evening, when we got to Brussels, Luo Qing flew to Taiwan, Germain stayed at a friend's house, and I stayed in a hotel. My room was on the second floor, right over the highway; whenever a car passed by the windowpanes rattled.

June 4, 1989, was a nightmare. I was in Berlin and stared at CNN the entire night, got stinking drunk. In the morning, a man from Beijing stumbled up the stairs to my room and threw his arms over my shoulder sobbing, "A girl on a balcony was shot dead. She was only seventeen. . . ." Such an image was especially painful for someone from Beijing.

I was utterly dejected by the events and gave Germain a call. The next day he rushed over from Spain and stayed with me for three days. I started to have second thoughts soon after he arrived—my English wasn't wonderful, and I was really in no mood for conversation.

That evening he treated me to dinner at an Italian restau-

rant. After ordering, he mentioned the vineyard and the region of a specific Italian wine, startling the waiter who then
quickly summoned the proprietor. The proprietor appeared
and chatted with him in Italian. Then he went down into the
cellar and returned with a 1969 bottle of this wine, opened it
for us himself, and poured some for Germain. He calmly
smelled it, swirled it in his glass, took a sip and swished it
around in his mouth, and, after a long while, with a bob of
his Adam's apple, the wine dropped into his stomach. "Not
bad," he eventually said, and the proprietor beamed at us.

Germain's manor has a wine cellar with some five thousand bottles of French, Italian, and Spanish wines. This
proves a degree of rationality, that he understands the value
of moderation and accumulation. If I were in charge of this
cellar, I'd probably drink myself to death. Germain told me
wine was one way he made money, and the key was knowing
the ropes. When he found a French wine with a mellow flavor,
he would buy four hundred bottles. Within two years, the
wine would go up a grade and the price would skyrocket.
Then he'd sell it off for a massive profit.

Germain is a born hedonist, and hedonists the world over
are much the same, sharing common themes—good wine,
good food, and love. By all accounts, he should be living quite
happily, but he perversely insisted on falling in love with that
most agonizing of things: poetry. Sometimes he complains to
me, "Look, here I am basking under the Mediterranean sun,
drinking Italian wine, eating French food, but I just can't
seem to write a poem." In my experience, being a poet requires some form of suffering, based either on your fate or
heart, and without a trace of either, it's difficult to write.

In addition to enjoying good food and wine, he can also

afford to travel the globe. Wherever there are poetry events, Germain's shadow can be found. But he swore to heaven that as long as I was unable to return to my own home, he would never visit China.

In the summer of 1990, Germain and I attended the World Congress of Poets in Seoul. Allen Ginsberg and the Russian poet Andrei Voznesensky were also there. Allen was bustling around and, as soon as I arrived, he grabbed me and held a press conference, requesting that the South Korean authorities release some poets they had locked up. I am a poor public speaker and my English was awful, so I magnanimously declined the potential embarrassment. Germain stood to the side, peering at us and shaking his mountain goat's beard as if he were practicing calligraphy with it. He told Allen that he didn't have sufficient understanding of the situation in South Korea and that his actions were too hasty. The two had just met and were already fighting. It took some courage for Germain to argue with Allen, whose mouth was twisted, his eyes bulging out in anger.

We also went to visit a Korean underground poet. This poet had spent many years in prison, and he spoke very quietly, as though always on guard against being followed or spied on. In a hotel room, he told us about the situations of many other underground poets.

I was scheduled to give a speech, but the organizing committee didn't provide me with a translator. With no other recourse, I stammered out the gist of what I wanted to say to Germain, and through gestures and a bit of guessing—and with the addition of Germain's own tone and point of view— he managed to write two full pages in English and read them for me at the meeting. It was the blind leading the blind, a blind Belgian leading a blind Chinese man passing through the light.

I am very grateful to Germain. In the course of my wanderings, especially in the icy world of northern Europe, his letters always brought warm Mediterranean greetings. Almost every time, he wrote at the bottom of his letter, "Dear friend, remember, Ithaca is your home, and you are always welcome in Ithaca!"

2

IN THE WINTER OF 1992, I was in the Netherlands and from there traveled to Ithaca. I had arranged things beforehand with Duo Duo, who left first with his Dutch girlfriend. I would arrive two days later. The Dutch winter is all freezing wind, miserable rain, and no sunlight. We used to go to an indoor pool and roast ourselves under the sunlamps, like chickens. Put in enough coins and you can bake for half an hour until you are cooked halfway through.

As soon as I got off the plane I broke into a wide smile— Mediterranean sunshine in every direction. Germain picked me up in a Mercedes and drove me around Alexander Harbor. Then we got on the toll highway. Because of the high tolls, cars were few and far between. The hills undulated and stretched out, cacti dozed in the sunlight, trees blackened by lightning flashed by. When we reached Altea, we followed a road that snaked up the mountain, eventually arriving at Ithaca Manor. The wrought iron gate automatically opened and our hostess, Liliane, called out to us as she held back three black dogs. She was the only other resident and treated Germain as if he were an emperor. When she looked at him, her eyes were full of admiration. In addition to money and leisure, the hedonist also requires such a wife.

The three dogs were extremely vicious, violent in temper, attacking friend and foe. When the locals saw them, they trembled, thus effectively preventing any thieves from worrying about Germain's riches. Ugly and cross-eyed, their tendons and muscles twitched under their skin.

This place definitely needed fearsome dogs at its gate for protection. Ithaca Manor occupies more than ten hectares of land, and there are hundreds of fruit trees of all kinds, including Chinese lichees. Flowers bloom in shifts all year long. In a letter, Germain wrote that there was always fruit you could pick and eat no matter what the season. It was no exaggeration. He had designed the house with a predominately Spanish flair. Antiques, originals and reproductions, were everywhere: Greek columns, Indian Buddhas, Chinese vases, African wood carvings—all coming across as a little chaotic. But this was just Germain's style, the result of his traveling the world. On the hillside, there was a gigantic aviary encaging a chair. Every morning, Germain would climb the hill, sit in the aviary, and read the newspaper. Pretty romantic until a bird shits on your head, dampening your mood for the day.

In the Mediterranean winter, it is seventy-seven degrees by noon. I lay on the veranda, stripped to the waist, chasing the Dutch dampness out of the crevices of my bones. Just as I was nodding off, Germain appeared, grinning, and dragged me off to work. He called me August Sleepwalker after one of my books of poems.

Germain was a workaholic. Besides writing poetry and translating, he also runs a small press, publishing five to ten volumes of poetry a year. His study is the main hall of Ithaca

Manor, facing the azure Mediterranean. We were working on the Chinese translation of a group of poems by Miguel Hernandez, one of Spain's most significant poets, whose tragic life ended in Franco's jail. Germain had mastered a number of languages, so he compared the original with the English, German, and Dutch translations. Sometimes, we would deliberate about one word until night trickled in.

Liliane loaded the table with food—silver utensils and crystal glasses reflected light off each other. Germain rubbed his hands, went to the wine cellar, and returned with a few bottles. After he had three glasses of wine, he berated the whining of contemporary poetry, brought up the "sensationism" advocated by the Portuguese poet Fernando Pessoa, and began shouting that he was going to start a new poetry movement. Duo Duo and I responded to his call in unison, and thus Neo-Sensacionismo was born at Ithaca Manor. No sooner was it announced that we set to work. Germain prepared an announcement, found a pen, ink, and a Japanese paper lantern, and had me write our slogan on it. Suddenly delirious, he rushed again to the wine cellar and brought back two bottles of wine he'd been saving for twenty years, and we raised our glasses to celebrate. I felt a bit unsteady and the Bodhisattvas and angels began to spin around us.

Early the next morning, Germain took us out on the road. We first went to Orihuela—the home of the poet Hernandez, not far from Ithaca. Our visit was in some ways a form of ancestor worship. His old home was poor and bare, no more than four walls, a roof, and a huge black and white portrait of the poet that looked out of place. He only lived thirty-eight years, yet he poured out poems of such brilliance.

Heading further south we drove straight to Granada, the home of Lorca: *Green, how much I want you green. / Green wind.*

Green branches. / The ship upon the sea. . . . Through Dai Wang-shu's translations, Lorca became the first teacher of our generation and had a lasting influence on our lives. His home was now a small museum with many precious objects, photographs, and music. The gaze in his photograph was sensitive and sad as it stared out at us from over half a century ago, during a time of war and suffering.

In southern Spain, one can see a singular blending of various cultures. The city of Granada was inhabited in the eighth century by Arabic-speaking North African Moors, whose rule lasted for five hundred years. The Alhambra, the symbol of Moorish civilization, is one of the most beautiful palaces in the world. How many Moorish spirits steered clear of the tourists, passing through the corridors and waterside pavilions, to disappear into secret stone doors?

The local flamenco with its dazzling costumes, lively rhythms, sensuousness, and passion is the crystallization of gypsy and Muslim culture in Andalusia. We drifted into a community center as dancers spun around the stage, the entire audience clapping a complex rhythm with different parts of their palms.

"You see, this is why I wanted to move to Spain!" Germain said with satisfaction. He urged me to move there as well and buy a small house near Ithaca. The idea interested me and I began counting up my economic resources on my fingers.

The Neo-Sensacionismo poetry movement could not simply rest where it was, and Germain began planning a poetry festival at Ithaca. He brought me to a round plaza near the sea—steps surrounded it, waves beat against the shore. This was to be the stage, with the audience in front and the setting sun behind. How would it be with musical accompaniment? Typical Germainesque romanticism.

I still thought he was just talking—a single individual does have some limits. But, to my surprise, this fellow mustered his car-selling skills and knocked on the doors of the bureaucrats, wheedling money out of their pockets. Three years later, in the spring of 1995, I returned to Ithaca where the curtain opened on the new La Costa Poetica Poetry Festival. Now Liliane was driven to exhaustion as she was secretary, accountant, driver, purchasing agent, cook, and tour guide. This must be the only poetry festival in the world run by a single couple.

When the festival was over, Liliane could only stare into space and Germain's laugh was empty.

Germain is always looking for new ways to do things. He initiated a "Planetary Awareness" international poetry program, then set up his "Anti-Pollution" poetry website, and I look on, knowing there is no way I can keep up with him. Nowadays, there aren't many people who take poetry as seriously.

I just received a letter from Germain. In it he writes that last year was, in terms of poetry, a bumper crop. In June, he attended the Rotterdam International Poetry Festival, then flew off to Italy. In August, he participated in the World Congress of Poets in the Czech Republic, and then left for Dublin because an Irish poet had invited him to read there. His collection of poems, *The Road*, and the illustrations for this book were exhibited at the Antwerp Book Fair in Belgium. He'd given seven readings in ten days. After that, Vienna . . .

At the end of the letter, he wrote about the gloomy political situation in China, and the peremptory behavior of the American Clinton Corporation, citing a line of his own poetry, "no shadow / is longer than its ray of light." Finally, he wrote, "The sun of Ithaca awaits you. . . ."

KING MARTIN

I

THE FIRST TIME I MET Martin was in early June 1985, in Berlin.
We met again soon after at the Rotterdam International Poetry
Festival. Martin was a little past fifty with a stocky, solid build,
and a bulging stomach. His hair was in mutiny against him—
graying and receding, a white flag after years of transformation. His mask-like smiling face was no facade but rather the
result of a long-held optimism. He founded the Rotterdam International Poetry Festival in 1970, and it has now become the
world's largest poetry festival. Full of good cheer, Martin has
been through more than twenty years of tunnels and the open
terrain of the imagination. He is not merely the chairman of
the festival, but the king of world poetry.

The small hotel we stayed at in downtown Rotterdam was
one of the only buildings that survived the Allied bombing in
World War II, and it still retained a pre-war style. On the walls
hung oil paintings of many-masted boats with brass steering
wheels. The sofas in the lobby were bulky and comfortable.
The doorman knew all the guests by name and chatted with
each of them. Every evening after the reading, the poets gathered at the hotel bar for a drink, thick tobacco smoke mixing
with all the different languages.

Martin assigned a young woman to interpret for me, and someone joked, "Bei Dao has a colorful butterfly circling him all the time." The young lady was mischievous and willful, translating a few words when she felt like it, but otherwise turning what I said on its head. At the time, my English was awful and I could only talk to Martin through her. Whether there was any communication between us was not really important, but I didn't want her to start cursing Martin for no apparent reason. It seems that my anxiety was unfounded, as Martin continued smiling and smiling without reservation.

After the festival, Martin let me spend the night at his house, and then offered to take me to the airport the next day. In the evening, he and his wife drove my interpreter and me to a castle for some beer. He was very excited and talked about his plans for the future. According to my interpreter, Martin said he wanted to invite even more Chinese poets to the festival, to introduce Dutch readers to their work. His face was ruddy, a danger sign at his age, and after speaking, he suddenly fell silent as if listening to his own answer. This was the first time I had been abroad, and everything was novel. I remember us sitting outside the bar, overhead burned Van Gogh's stars. I drank so much that my tongue grew thick and my speech slurred, and I smiled like an idiot along with Martin. I stood up and weaved my way to the toilet, all the tables covered with glasses of beer swirling away.

When I visited Martin again—as an exile—I asked him to take me back to the castle for another drink, but he couldn't remember what I was talking about.

In 1987, I moved to Durham, England, with my family to teach Chinese at a university. In the spring of 1988, Martin and his assistant, Joke, traveled to London on business and wanted to visit us. The north of England was still very cold and dreary, and the train was more than an hour late, forcing me, during my miserable wait, to stuff ten pounds in a slot machine. Martin and Joke were both wearing cream-colored jackets, like a veterinarian and his assistant. At this point, I was finally able to converse with them in my own stammering English. Martin spoke English with a thick, guttural tone, as if he was drinking some bitter medicinal brew. They had to take a train back that same day so they could only stay two or three hours. We sat down around a pot of tea. Joke looked like your typical Dutch woman—red face, high cheekbones, and she smiled abruptly at Martin's prompting. In spite of the English sense of her name, she was quite serious. They wanted to see some of Shao Fei's paintings. The pictures were set out one by one, and in-between English expressions of appreciation, they murmured in Dutch. Finally, Martin solemnly announced that he would invite both of us to Rotterdam and hold a show of her work during the next poetry festival.

Summer came early that year as the numerous photographs of our daughter, Tiantian, prove. She was only three. In one picture taken in front of a windmill, she's wearing a yellow and white checkered dress and is frowning; in another picture, several poets are playing with her on a tour boat in Rotterdam Harbor; and then there is one where Shao Fei is holding her inside the Van Gogh Museum and Tiantian is showing her front teeth, like a little rabbit. . . . Of course, these details of my life have nothing to do with King Martin, who belonged to everyone, who belonged to that holy land called poetry. The poetry festival opened and, like a moving target, Martin never stayed in one place for long, grinning from ear to ear, eyes wide open but seeing no one, waving and saying hello to people who were there and people who weren't. I knew this was due to fatigue. Just think about the dozens of bureaucrats and businessmen who dug into their own pockets for this festival, the scores of high-maintenance poets, and on top of that, the more than a thousand picky spectators. When Chairman Mao met with the Red Guards, he just waved his hands like he was shooing away a fly, but none dared get too close to him.

The Chinese poets that year were Ma Gaoming, Shu Ting, and I. Along with the Dutch sinologist Michiel van Crevel, Ma Gaoming had translated a recently published anthology of contemporary Dutch poetry. For some reason, Ma Gaoming didn't get his visa until the very last minute and, with his new bride, hurriedly boarded a Swissair flight that cost more than twenty thousand Swiss francs. When they tried to get their tickets reimbursed by the poetry festival, it was as if they burned the hands of whoever touched them. They were ignored by everyone, creating an intense dispute among the organizers, and roused the sleepwalking Martin. With some sort of sixth sense, he was able to steer clear of anyone Chinese. If I wanted to find Martin to talk to him about something, he would suddenly turn a corner when he was still five or ten meters away, raise his hands, and greet a row of columns.

2

AT THE TIME OF THE Tiananmen Square massacre, I was in Berlin. Whenever Martin wrote or phoned, he would express his condolences and then ask endless questions about the fate of the Chinese writers who were being persecuted. He said that he and his colleagues were exerting all their influence to get poets around the world to help their Chinese comrades. At the 1990 festival, the annual prize in the imprisoned poets category was given to the Chinese poet Song Lin and accepted on his behalf by a Romanian poet. The awards ceremony was grave and dignified, handled more like a memorial service. Martin put aside his smile, like a minister praying for a departed soul. Actually, due to communication difficulties, the poet himself had already slipped out of the coffin, and at that very moment was riding his bicycle beneath laundry hanging in the back alleys of Shanghai.

Emphasizing the close tie between poetry and politics was the basis of King Martin's national strategy. For a Dutch person, this was doubtlessly the correct policy: following the premises of Western humanism, he treasured the human voice and struggled against the powers that tried to silence it. Sadly, there is no so-called "universal truth." And from the point of view of many who have been rescued, true resistance lies in allowing poetry to separate itself from politics, leaving behind the language of states and thus freeing itself from the vicious circle of history. These misunderstandings between East and West sometimes exist in tacit accord, and are sometimes a cruel joke, embarrassing both sides.

At this moment, sitting at my desk, I try to recall an image of Martin but suddenly I feel lost. I've taken part in four poetry festivals and one writers' festival in the Netherlands, and have also lived there for ten months, but the impressions Martin has left me with are fragmented and contradictory. He was over fifty when I met him, and I have no proof that he had ever been younger. Furthermore, time during the poetry festival didn't count as Martin was surrounded by the public and wouldn't have acknowledged his own mother. And even when it was just the two of us, he didn't talk about himself. His private life was hidden behind a curtain, and when the curtain went up, everything was all tidied away for him to greet the audience.

I remember this scene: Getting off the train in Rotterdam, I walk through the train station plaza, make two turns among the tall buildings downtown, and arrive at a quiet, empty theater. The offices of the poetry festival occupy one corner and are piled high with posters and brochures. Martin comes out to greet me and hugs me tightly. He hugs in the French style, and is not satisfied until he gnaws both cheeks. I am the taller and have to bend down to keep my balance. The annual poetry festival has not yet begun. Martin's head is clear, his talk is cheerful and good-natured, but the best thing is he knows who I am, something that is important above all else to a guest. After asking about the situation in China and about the health of my family, he mysteriously draws forth a letter. It is five sheets of dense scribbles from Ma Gaoming. Ma wants to organize a large delegation in Beijing that would go to Rotterdam just to wave their flags and raise their battle cries. Haltingly, Martin says, "He's crazy, he's crazy." But one can see he's praising Ma Gaoming from his heart—without such madness, it would have been absolutely impossible for Martin to organize a poetry festival like Rotterdam.

Martin always maintained good relations with bureau-crats and businessmen. This was the key to the success of his poetry festival. He has invited them to speak at the opening ceremonies, given them the best seats, drank with them, ate with them, and catered to them. But Martin has his own set of principles. For example, though he wears a suit, he never wears a tie. This is a kind of status marker, signifying his stance with the dressed down poets. The queen of Holland once wanted to receive him, and the palace staff notified him that his dress was to be formal, which included a tie. Martin refused the invitation. Later, the queen found out about this and issued a special order allowing him the favor of appearing before her without a tie.

Having written this far, I am seized by an impulse and, after rummaging through boxes and cabinets, I find Martin's telephone number. "Hello," his voice is weak. I make him guess who I am and listen to him fumble around, until I confess who I am. He cries out in surprise, as if his house has just caught on fire, "Bei Dao? Is that you? I have been trying to track you down!" After a few words of polite conversation, he begins again with the same old story: "I asked an old Chinese poet where Bei Dao was. He answered 'Bei Dao doesn't exist, because he isn't in our system.' But you see, I've found you. . . ." His happiness is the happiness of discovery. I change the subject, and ask about his life. "You know, retirement is a difficult thing, I've also started a new foundation called Poets of All Nations. . . . This June we went to Colombia. It's a very poor place, but eight thousand people came to hear one reading! Just unbelievable." Martin grows more forceful as he speaks; poetry festivals are the motivating force in his life. He tells me that he is going to China next month and that he will see Ma Gaoming in Beijing. "He is editing a very thick directory of international poetry festivals funded by our foundation. Of course, I still remember those two plane tickets; that was a big topic for us. Yes, he is still drinking as much as ever. But that doesn't matter, his ideas are still good. . . ."

3

RETIREMENT IS A REAL SORE point for Martin. I found a fax he sent me two years ago: "Perhaps you know that I have left the International Poetry Festival due to considerations of age. Last year, after the twenty-seventh festival, I turned sixty-six, and in this country you have to stop working by sixty, or at sixty-five at the latest, so I had no choice but to leave. . . ." Between the lines, he sighed with each step.

From October 1992 to the summer of 1993, I was writer-in-residence at the University of Leiden. This position was specifically created for writers in exile, and Martin was one of those who pushed for it. By American standards, Leiden and Rotterdam would be considered two districts of the same city as it's only a forty-minute train ride between them. But I seldom went to see Martin, first because he was a busy man, and also because I was not getting on well with myself at the time and was in no mood to go dropping in on people. Mostly we just called each other. Martin had a fixed program: he always first asked about my family and China, and then he would bring up the main topic.

I recall that in the spring of 1993, I made a special trip to Rotterdam to see Martin and arranged to have lunch with him. We went to an authentic Cantonese restaurant near the poetry festival's office. Joke joined us, her face a moon reflecting the light of Martin's sun. We talked as we ate. As Martin warmed up to the conversation, he became more pleased, and yet again he brought out the letter from Ma Gaoming for me to see—the proof of his youth. He and Joke saw me to the train. The sun was warm, and the many Dutch people who had survived the bitter winter wind and rain were walking around the train station plaza. Martin suddenly said that he was old and had diabetes. I said, "You should retire." Martin turned to me, his eyebrows raised in surprise with a queer expression on his face, coarse white whiskers popping out of his cheeks, and he stared at me as if checking to see if I was plotting against him. "Yes, it's a good idea," he said with a bitter laugh, "but I have got plenty of energy, and what will I do if I retire?" He was right. How can the king retire? Martin had been on the throne for twenty-seven years and was deposed in the Year of Our Lord nineteen hundred and ninety-six.

Considering the various rumors circulating about Martin's retirement, I would have preferred to remain in the dark. His successor was a young woman with a Russian name, Tatjana. Her name, she told me, was the result of her father's love for the poetry of Pushkin. We had met two years earlier at the Paris Poetry Festival. She was a modern professional—shrewd and competent, dynamic and vigorous, totally different from Martin's style. King Martin was deposed by a democratic system, driven away by the dominant trend that could not be stopped. I heard that Martin was not content to let his deposition rest—he wanted to establish another international poetry festival and stake a rival claim to the territory. I was truly sad for Martin, and wanted to write him a letter urging him to give up any plans to restore himself to the throne. But nowadays, who can convince anyone of anything?

All power corrupts and absolute power corrupts absolutely. This was taught to me in English in the summer of 1992 by Michiel van Crevel who was interpreting for me at the Rotterdam Poetry Festival. It was mostly a tongue twister.

Towards the end of King Martin's reign, various expressions of dissatisfaction had already begun to be heard. At first their voice was weak—the buzzing of a few flies—but it gradually grew into a roar. I believe Martin neither heard nor saw anything. During the poetry festival he played blind man's bluff. It reminded me of a line by the Finnish poet Edith Sodergran: "the marvelous solitude of the throne."

Each year, Martin's opening ceremony speech grew longer and longer. Between the clichés, hackneyed expressions, and his muddy pronunciation, it was enough to put people to sleep. In addition, his wife and son both started out as volunteer workers at the poetry festival, then gradually approached the center of power. And there was another criticism: some believed that poets who were invited were all old friends of Martin, that the poetry festival had become something of a family reunion. If that was the case, then I was a beneficiary. But actually, one of the festival's founding principles was to allow certain poets to regularly reappear to see how their work changed over time.

If you mention a famous poet, Martin will know him. So-and-so was still a young hothead, so-and-so has died, so-and-so won the Nobel Prize, so-and-so just came to see me. . . . Nobody was beyond Martin, and many poets were his personal discoveries. He always had good things to say about other people, with the exception of Derek Walcott. "His poetry is not bad, but he is much too demanding," Martin said to me. One year at the poetry festival, Martin's son, Marc, went to the airport to pick Walcott up and take him to his hotel. For the sake of convenience, Marc parked the car in the hotel parking lot, but Walcott flew into a rage and insisted that Marc bring the car to the front door.

I would really like to have known the younger Martin, Martin before he became king. What color was his hair? What kind of laugh did he have? What were his dreams for poetry? I know many Dutch poets, all of whom are friends of Martin. I should go ask them about the young Martin, but I'm afraid there'd be all kinds of conflicting stories, even about things like the color of his hair. Martin has had a rich range of experiences: night school teacher, employee at a publishing house, manager of a bookstore, editor of a literary magazine, newspaper critic, translator of quite a few German literary works, and editor of several international poetry anthologies. In 1969, he joined the Rotterdam Arts Committee, power shifted, and the gates for his poetry festival opened. Résumés, though, are always suspect. They are only a formality and don't have much relationship to life and the actual person.

"Looking back, I think Martin has done so many important things," I once said to Michiel van Crevel during a long-distance phone call.

"You don't need to convince me, I know all about his accomplishments. . . ." he replied a little impatiently.

"No, I was trying to convince myself."

BACKYARD

THE WIND IS PICKING UP. I stand at the window looking helplessly at the four orange trees in my backyard and the three wild trees leaning over the wall, their leaves cascading into my swimming pool. This causes endless labor, dredging out one batch of leaves as another falls. It would be one thing if it was fish or dollars, but the only result of my battle with nature is a heap of rotten leaves.

Still, I like my backyard, a private space and the polar opposite of my front lawn. Front lawns are most likely the result of a collusion between the FBI and real estate developers—an effort to standardize the thought patterns of average American citizens. A kind of dialogue exists among lawns, and like foreigners living in an English-language environment, unkempt lawns are always beaten in an argument. When the grass in your lawn grows tall and turns brown, both the smooth green lawns and their owners reproach you. Puffing and panting, you're forced to furiously push the lawn mower, especially during the dog days of summer when the grass leaps up as soon as you turn your back.

Our lawn mower is secondhand and has problems with its starter. After gathering up my strength, I yank the cord hard a few dozen times, but nothing happens. Sweat has already begun to flow down my neck. I strip to the waist and pull some more. The lawn mower finally coughs once, then emits black smoke. I must look hopeless, and I imagine the neighbors must watch the show from behind their curtains.

Sometimes I sit in the rocking chair in the backyard and watch the sky rock. This chair, bought four years ago when we moved, was assembled with great difficulty. The tree rings on the rounded wooden supporting frame used to revolve with the years and shine in the sunlight. It looked like a brand new gibbet, and sitting on it, you felt a certain degree of uneasiness. Now, the elements have discolored the rocking chair and it's covered with dust and dirt. It no longer has many customers.

When we bought this house, we were immediately taken with the swimming pool. The water was clear, blue, and inspired longing, so without even looking at a second place we sealed the deal, probably the first time such a thing has happened in the history of real estate transactions in this city. Who would have dreamed that this swimming pool would exact such a price? In addition to dredging up all the leaves from seven trees in the winter, I must also clean out innumerable ants, moths, worms, snails, water bugs, and dragonflies who probably mistook the water for sky. In Air Force jargon this is called "the deep blue," dreaded by every flyer. Even though there are underwater vacuum cleaners, every machine still requires a human being to wait on it. You have to dig the dirt out of the vacuum cleaner bag, wash the filter, adjust the timer, and always keep up with the maintenance and repairs of the circulation system. Besides this, the pool water has to be kept at the right pH, or else the walls of the pool will grow algae and insects will breed in it. Not long ago, I was away for two weeks and left my parents in charge of the house. When I came back the swimming pool was well on its way to becoming a swamp.

There is a mighty kingdom of ants in our backyard, and from time to time this kingdom attacks our house, especially during the cold, dismal winters. First, they send a small, silent team on a reconnaissance mission to scout the way. No one notices them, so the army makes a drive into the house, forcing us to use great quantities of biological weapons to exterminate them. This canned ant poison is quite insidious as it looks like hawthorn jelly and is no doubt sweet and tasty. When I put it in the path of the ants, droves of worker ants bring it back to the queen as a sign of their devotion—and the queen's subsequent death by poison means no more children or grandchildren. In theory, this is how it should work. After placing a number of these cans around the house and counting out the days as predicted by the directions, I notice that the kingdom of ants has shown no sign of decline, and is in fact thriving. I guess that the queen has long ago built up a resistance to the poison, and is by now perhaps even addicted to it and can't bear to part with her dessert. But human sympathy has its limits. I've never heard of a group for the protection of ants established anywhere. As for their social attributes, ants and humans are similar to each other. After seeing the animated movie *Antz*, I was truly moved to deep compassion. But soon afterward there was another onslaught of the ant army, and I had to harden my heart against them again.

Unlike ants, spiders are the representatives of a solitary and gloomy world. In this respect they are a bit like philosophers, relying on their tightly woven webs for sustenance. They can move up or down, meeting success whichever way they move, settling down to the business of life in corners and

crannies, under eaves, and among twigs. One day a workman
came to do some maintenance on our swimming pool. When
he opened the round plastic filter cover, he gasped, and with a
few cruel blows of his screwdriver, stabbed a spider to death.
He flipped it over for me to see the red mark on the black
widow's abdomen.

2

SPRING FOLLOWED WINTER AND A pair of swallows have
made their nest in our yard, a fact discovered by my daughter.
Watching through the sliding glass door, we could see a great
building project underway beneath the eaves. The two swallows put in extra hours, carrying mud and blades of grass,
gluing the stuff together with their saliva. This is similar
to the bird's nest soup that we eat, but the difference lies in
the fact that the nests used in genuine bird's nest soup are
built on sheer stone cliffs on the seacoast, and the building
material is made of saliva, fish-spawn, and seaweed. The swallows worked on the nest for a week. My background is in construction work. Out of a vague sense of collegial rivalry,
I strolled slowly around it and had to admit a feeling of
admiration—this was a house accomplished by mouths alone.
Though from an architectural point of view, the nest was only
a terrace, since it relied on the eaves to protect it from wind
and rain.

The process of incubation is soundless, like writing a
poem, and one must overcome unhelpful impatient moods.
Separated from the nest of swallows by a thin pane of glass,
I was bent over my computer, stuck between some frag-

mented lines of poetry, when suddenly my daughter called me downstairs—two baby swallows had hatched. The father and mother were busy carrying food in their beaks, flying back and forth. The baby swallows had their eyes closed and their mouths wide open, squeaking piteously.

What really threatened their existence were our two cats, Haku and Mata. Added together, their age was equivalent to an adult human: "at thirty I was established." They cherished no ambitions. Besides, there were no mice for them to catch—and a boring world it was with no mice! When American cats get together, they generally just yawn and sigh. After a few generations, the genes they pass on have probably mutated so the cats have no reaction at all when they see a mouse, or maybe even run away from it. Haku and Mata doze the day away, sometimes stepping outside for a stroll. They have their own little cat door set into our big human door. While my fear of thieves prevents other people from coming through our door, the cats pass in and out freely.

I've come to realize the cats are the real masters of the backyard. They go to the bathroom on the lawn, roll in the mud, drink and admire their reflections in the swimming pool, and climb up on the wooden fence to watch the sunset. Over the past two years, Haku has put on weight, and is not as nimble as before. But Mata has an amazing talent—with just a gentle leap, she can reach the top of the wooden fence, which is as tall as a person, and with another jump, shoot onto the roof. For the first two years after our move, these two often brought home little birds, dragonflies, locusts, and other such creatures and expected a reward for their accomplishments, getting instead a harsh scolding, or even a good stiff beating. In their eyes, human beings are probably totally irrational. Eventually the cats omitted the final step from their procedure and settled for eating their kill a little ways off from us. We still often find sparrow feathers in the backyard proving that American sparrows are foolish, unlike their Chinese cousins. I remember once on the outskirts of Beijing, as I raised my air rifle at some sparrows on an electrical wire from a hundred paces away, they flapped their wings and flew away.

American swallows are different. After all, they have the benefit of extensive migrations, so they have seen a thing or two. First they survey the territory, then build a nest somewhere well out of the reach of cat claws. By the time it was summer, the baby swallows had grown up and their parents were teaching them to fly. Soon their terrace was too crowded, and one morning they all left the nest and never returned, probably in search of a warmer place. I went back to my desk with an empty heart.

The lady of the house went away and the twenty-some roses that she had tended quickly withered. I thought rose bushes were hardy plants and simply bloomed continuously. But they all died at once like a lightbulb, making the yard dark. Every other day, I dragged out the hose to water them. In addition to watering, roses need to be pruned, fertilized, and sprayed with insecticide. I never really liked roses—one false move and they scratch you, causing pain that bores straight into your heart. I have often fallen prey to their plots and try to steer clear of them.

With the roses extinguished, the yard has again brightened by the four orange trees loaded with brilliant golden fruit. I don't know if they are the wrong variety, or if they are not sufficiently cared for, but the oranges taste sour, sour enough to make your teeth ache. So we just leave them on the tree for the wind to blow off; the stubborn ones hang on till the next summer and get to meet the new generation. One of the four trees is actually a grapefruit tree and hardly makes its presence known; it only produces two large fruit each year, like the great udders of a cow. And the fruit was all dried out inside, like cotton batting.

In the southwest corner of the yard, a grape vine is on the verge of crushing its supporting arbor. The shoots were given to me by a friend, and I casually planted them in the corner without thinking much about it. Who would have suspected that two years of silent growth could have produced so much? For a while I worried that one day they would spread from the arbor to the house, covering everything and crushing our home. Looking more carefully at its tendrils, I can see they are like the tiny hands of bureaucrats, clutching any possibility in order to climb higher. The desire for growth and the desire for power are similar, except power doesn't bear fruit. When the grapes are ripe, they hang down in bunches, heavy and full, with no one to eat them, rotting on the vine. I recall a fragment from a poem by Shi Zhi I memorized thirty years ago: "When my purple grapes are transformed into the tears of deep autumn. . . ."

The sky grows cloudy. Outside the window I see Haku taking a stroll in the yard. His belly sags down, but when he walks, he still has the majesty of a tiger, head held high, striding proudly along, shaking his fur coat slightly. A gust of wind blows, stirs the seven trees, leaves and fruit tumble into the swimming pool startling Haku, causing him to turn his tail and flee.

COUNTRY MOUSE

I

THE CHILDREN'S STORY GOES like this: A country mouse invites a city mouse to visit him in the country and feeds him corn, potatoes, and grain. After eating, the city mouse doesn't say a word except to invite the country mouse to visit him in the city. One day, the country mouse goes to the city. He is surprised to find that the city mouse eats ten times better than him: cheese, butter, ham, cake, and such fare. But right in the middle of stuffing themselves, the city mouse cries out, "Run for your life! It's the cat!" He scrambles away, but having escaped that danger, he is almost crushed beneath one of the many cars flying back and forth along the street. Finally, panting for breath, the country mouse says, "I am better off with my peaceful life in the country. Here you may eat well, but you fear for your life all the time."

I am a country mouse who enjoys looking up at the blue sky and white clouds all day. But I was a city mouse for many decades before this, wandering all over the world: "At forty, I was no longer confused." Five years ago, I moved to a small town in California and finally settled down. Every time I go back to the city, I eat and drink well, but I miss the quiet of the country.

Compared to Beijing, our little town is the countryside. There are fifty thousand or so people living here, and no industry other than a tomato processing plant. Surrounded on all sides by fields, you'd ride a horse to death before reaching the distant mountains. The agricultural school of the University of California at Davis is ranked number one or two in the U.S., but because the university uses animals in experiments, it is frequently attacked by the local Greenpeace group. Bicycles are the main means of transportation in town. There is no news in the local paper, and the daily air pollution index is so low that it creates the illusion that I'm living on another planet.

Every day I wake up to the calling of birds. Listening carefully, I can make out the exaggerated flirting of two red-billed tits; a magpie chatters away in a one-way dialogue; a flock of sparrows acts like a bunch of unruly fellows, afraid they won't get the attention they deserve.

In Paris, I woke at exactly 2:00 a.m. every night when the bar across the street closed and tossed out the drunks who moaned and howled outside my window. At 6:25 a.m., I was awakened again by the garbage truck, and though I would immediately cover my ears with the pillow, it was no use. The truck was as heavy as a tank, making noises that shocked me into panicked wakefulness, crashing around as if it was trying to come directly into my bedroom, pack me in, and take me away. It reminded me of when I was a child living in Sanbulao Alley in Beijing, across the street from a textile plant. In the summer, all the windows of the plant were opened like a hundred loudspeakers shouting at us in some monotone language. The factory closed on Fridays, but the silence unbearable. At night I would toss and turn, wishing they would hurry up and get back to work.

But this was nothing compared to the noise in New York. I once stayed at a friend's house in downtown Manhattan. In the middle of the night, I was awakened by the crisp, clean sound of gunshots, closely followed by the approaching howl of sirens. The next morning I read in the newspaper that it had been an exchange of fire between some gangsters—one dead and two wounded. When you bring this up with New Yorkers, they complain that you are overreacting.

But don't forget that New Yorkers have grown up in a hail of gunfire that has toughened their nerves. They say that when someone fires a gun on the street, most New Yorkers, with as much experience as any guerilla, will just lower their heads, crouch slightly, and step clear of any possible danger. Then they might curse a little, brush the dust off their clothes, stand up straight, and rush back to their own battlefields.

One night in Paris I was robbed. It was after eleven and a friend had just dropped me off at the place where I was staying near the Gare de l'Est. I noticed two men following me—one tall, one short. The short one scuttled forward a couple of steps until he was at my side. In halting English he said, "Money! We have guns." I cast a glance behind me, the big one put his hand inside of his jacket, but it didn't really look like he had a gun; it could just as easily have been the stump of a broomstick. I fumbled around and dug out one hundred fifty francs. They snatched the money and ran off. The next day, I passed by a bar in the neighborhood and saw the two off-duty thieves drinking with my francs.

On his first visit to New York, a Danish sinologist I know was standing on a street in Manhattan holding a map, looking around him, when suddenly a large black man put a friendly arm around his shoulders and the point of a knife in the small of his back. Trapped, he could only pull some money out of the pocket of his shirt. At first he thought he could get rid of the mugger by just giving him five or ten dollars. But he accidentally pulled out a one hundred dollar bill. The man seized his wrist. The dire circumstances inspired my friend to rail bitterly about racial discrimination in the U.S. The man was pleased and gave him a discount, lowering his price to eighty dollars. Then my friend started cursing president Reagan, calling him all manner of foul names. The black man clapped him on the shoulder—"Brother, you're cool, just give me fifty." The sinologist and thief shook hands, parting reluctantly.

Running into a mugger with such a friendly disposition was a stroke of luck, though naturally it is best not to run into them at all. Starting in the eighties, students from China surged into big American cities in great numbers. Poor, they could only live in the worst areas. When faced with danger, they each developed their own clever stratagems. I met a foreign Chinese student in New York who would dress in a very special way: black wool overcoat, sunglasses, black fedora pushed down over his eyes, cigarette hanging askew from his mouth. With both hands in his pockets, he'd skulk crabwise down the street—a typical FBI agent from a Hollywood movie of the thirties or forties. Even though his outfit was a little out of date, it still struck fear in the hearts of evildoers, who did their best to keep their distance.

Dali was my classmate in high school. He has studied in New York for four years and lives in Harlem. I asked him how he was able to survive the constant warfare without having so much as a hair on his head harmed. "You must have extraordinary kung fu skills," I guessed. He shook his head mysteriously, spread out his fingers, and summarized three things he had learned: "First, when you see a group of suspicious-looking figures, adopt a cowering attitude, cross the street and go around them. Second, if you can't avoid them, look right into the face of the one who looks like he might be the leader, and let him know you will remember him; this will reduce the impulse to commit a crime. The third, and most crucial, is that whenever somebody is following you, you must head to the nearest garbage can and start rummaging around in it." I didn't comprehend this final point. Dali said with a chuckle, "If you are poorer than him, why would he rob you?"

2

THE FAMOUS RUSSIAN CELLIST Mstislav Rostropovich once said that city people are in a race toward death. This is a sensible observation. City mice are exhausted every day from being constantly on the run, as if they're wound up on a spring. Except for sleeping, when do they have time to rest? Actually, life is a kind of experiencing—if there's no time for leisure, how can one's experience deepen? Time filled compresses. A year seems as short as a day and rushes by.

But we have entertainment, say the city mice. But entertainment is empty. Like work, it fills time and cannot bring true leisure. People get together because they are afraid of loneliness. And besides, nowadays, if you want to see a movie, you don't have to live in the city. A lot of people, trying to appear sophisticated, go to great lengths to see the first screening of a new movie so as to have some conversational capital when they see their coworkers the next day. But what I really don't understand is why city people get so meticulously dressed up to go listen to classical music. After all, they aren't going to a wedding reception. And then once there, you pay for your own punishment—stifling coughs and holding bladders, not even daring to breathe too loud. If you aren't careful and doze off, you'll be wakened by the applause. Then you stand up with everyone else and cheer without stopping until the musicians come back out for an encore. Isn't this ridiculous? Listening to music is a private affair. It's better to stay at home and not make such a big fuss.

But we country mice . . .

My New York friend Eliot teases me right back saying, "Country mouse? What you are is a suburban mouse."

Generally speaking, suburban mice work themselves to death, drive Camrys, eat fast food, tighten their belts so they can afford to live in a good school district, borrow money to buy a house, cut grass and tend flowers, go running, and walk the dog; behind closed doors they watch TV, argue, and burn themselves out, then spend money to see a psychiatrist.

After careful consideration, there aren't many real country mice in the United States. Most are suburban mice, workaholics not really much better off than city mice at all. According to recent statistics, Americans work the longest hours in the world, even surpassing the Japanese, who are notorious workaholics. What people call the wealth of America seems to me to be nothing but a number; all day Americans are pointlessly busy; butts in the air chasing their own shadows. After they earn all that money, what then? When is there time to enjoy any of it?

The layout and structure of a house in some ways determines how people live. Gazing out over the suburbs, most of the houses look like they've been formed from the same mold. Over time, the people living inside also become exactly the same as each other. Having taught at universities, I've found that American kids all think in more or less the same way, which at first surprised me. But then after staring at row upon row of standardized houses in the suburbs, I understood why. Sometimes I think this kind of modernized brainwashing is more frightening than authoritarian brainwashing because people can lose their awareness of resistance and begin to think that everything is exactly as it should be.

Americans are in love with the idea of space—the bigger the better—from big houses, big cars, and big TVs, to eating big, drinking big, and getting big. There are many fat people in the suburbs, directly related to the piles of junk food they consume. Every weekend I drive my car and join the ranks of American shoppers. Chain stores like Costco are as large as an airport, and the merchandise looks like it's just been unloaded from an airplane. All the food comes in bulk packaging: ten pounds of beef, five dozen eggs, thirty cans of beer. Cars are stuffed full, each person goes home overflowing with happiness.

A South African friend of mine visited the U.S. and said to me with surprise, "Americans are so poor they are fattened to death." Mulling over this comment, I realized it had two implications: first, American obesity, in general, is a result of the wide ranks of the working people who are too hungry to be picky; second, it refers to the coarseness of the culinary culture in the United States. This must have something to do with the traditions of the Puritans whose descendants happened to become wealthy very rapidly, wanted more and more faster and faster. So they made processed junk food wrapped in commercial packaging and then spread it all over the world along with their advertising. When American monsters like McDonalds and KFC can gain a foothold in China—where people never tire of seeking the most exquisite kinds of food—you can see just how formidable they are.

The worst are American-style buffets in small towns that draw fat people in droves. I think this is one of the most fiendish parts in the plot of commercialization. Like opium addiction, it makes people who like to eat unable to stop even if they want to, fattening them until it kills them.

Writing this, I cannot suppress a shiver. Is suburban life really so horrible? I think suburban mice at least put on the appearance of civility. In the morning, when you go out for a walk, people wave and greet you with endless hellos and good mornings. After all, this is better than city mice with their cross faces and cold manners, always ready to draw knives on each other. They say that if a child from the country first visiting New York gets off the bus and greets each passing pedestrian, no one will pay any attention, and before long, the child will give up. Maybe in the big city people have a deeper understanding of loneliness and don't need to pretend otherwise. If not, then they're nothing more than Giacometti's statues—people as thin as bamboo rods set in the metropolis.

New York City is a lunatic asylum. I was in New York two days ago, staying with a friend who lives in Greenwich Village. It was the middle of the night when we went out and New York's nightlife had just begun—the throngs of traffic and blazing lights and colors made me gape. A young woman was shouting in the street, talking to a man over the parked cars; an old man, most likely just out of jail, was running laps in the same place; a half-naked drunk stood muttering to himself in the street; a tall, wiry black man walked along, swinging his hips, moving his hands to a rhythm only he could hear.

While writing this, I'm suddenly aware that I've most definitely become a country mouse and it would be very difficult for me to readjust to city life. But then new changes have also happened in my life. This country mouse has no choice but to move back to New York, that most odious of places. I must prepare myself for air pollution and noise, fear and the art of survival.

DRINKING STORIES

IT'S LATE. I TURN OFF THE LIGHT and sit down by the fireplace, open a bottle of red wine, and savor it while listening to the sound of the wind and while watching the fire blaze. This is the most relaxing part of my day.

The culture of drinking differs from culture to culture. A Chinese hermit and a French aristocrat have completely different attitudes toward their wine. Sunlight, soil, and fruit are all transformed into cultural codes when alcohol dissolves into the blood. So don't bother trying to find English equivalents for Chinese adjectives that describe wine, such as *chunhou* ("full and mellow") and *mian* ("soft and lingering"), and vice versa. I once accompanied two American drinking connoisseurs to Napa. They piously raised their glasses to let the sunlight pass through the wine, then took a sip, sloshed it around in their mouths, spat it out, and then spat out a great string of wine jargon. I think most of this terminology is derived from the French but in the process of translation was simplified by the Puritan's coarse drinking habits. Translatability depends on the rationality of the thing. For the most part, irrational things like wine, like humor, can't be translated.

Ancient civilizations have been divided into two broad classes: the Dionysian and the Apollonian. Chinese culture originally could have been placed in the category of civilization named after the god of wines. The Xia and Shang were drunken dynasties—"pools of wine and forests of meat." The rulers drank and the common people drank, many drinking themselves to death. They say that because lamp oil was expensive at that time, most places were unlit at night, so what else was there to do but drink? Later, these dynasties inevitably fell to a more sober dynasty, the Zhou. The Duke of Zhou advocated "creating rituals and establishing music." Once they abandoned wine, the cultural genes of the Chinese people changed accordingly.

I can't hold much liquor, but I'm an avid drinker nonetheless. This seems to have something to do with my early experiences of hunger. During the famine years of 1959–1962, I often went to a bar near my home to buy cold snacks. Food was in short supply, and the bar changed its rules: You could not buy any of the cold snacks without buying a glass of beer. I was only ten then. To this day, I still remember that little shop, located on the corner of a T-intersection in the Ping'an neighborhood of Beijing. Its door and windows were pale blue. It was filthy, and inside there were only two small tables and a few stools. Many plates of cold snacks were stacked within a tall glass case. I would hand over a crumpled bill, take my plate of food and empty it into an aluminum lunch box, and then, carefully carrying the glass of beer, stand in the doorway to watch the passing cars. The beer was chilled and had a mildewy flavor. On the way back home, my legs would feel rubbery and I could not walk in a straight line. At the time, I had not yet experienced the advantages of alcohol; I simply saw it as the price I had to pay to avoid hunger.

The first time I got really drunk was at the beginning of the Cultural Revolution. My classmates and I went hiking up a mountain near Zhoukoudian outside of Beijing. We spent the night camping on the side of the mountain in a spot out of the wind. It was April and cold, "the gauze quilt cannot stand up to the fifth-watch cold," as the poet Li Yu wrote. We couldn't sleep, and everyone sat in a circle in the moonlight, shivering. Someone produced two bottles of cheap wine, which were passed around the circle. I drank eagerly on an empty stomach and got drunk very quickly. That drunkenness was unforgettable. In the mountain wilds, with the shades of evening raging, and the stars bursting wide open, I floated around as if I were becoming an otherworldly immortal, heroic sentiments towering skyward. I wonder if the passion of those who are called revolutionaries is based on this sort of intoxication, a desire to be free from the limits of petty life and the mundane world, a desire to devote oneself to a great cause.

If intoxication is like an ascension to heaven, then getting dead drunk is like descending into hell. I haven't gotten dead drunk very often because I usually fall asleep first. I suspect this is an instinctual form of self-preservation. I know myself, and before drinking, I survey the territory, only relaxing if there is a bed or sofa.

In the spring of 1986, Shao Fei and I traveled to Inner Mongolia, and some friends took us to visit some people on the steppes. The people there have simple, unaffected customs, and the only way to entertain guests is by drinking and singing. So we alternated singing and drinking, then drank after we sang and sang after we drank, until we finally all collapsed. Yurts are very convenient. You simply lay back and fall asleep in the earth's embrace. When I woke up, I remained very still and played dead so that I wouldn't have to drink until I passed out again. Mongolians are an honorable people and don't check your blood alcohol level like the American police. If you are no longer sitting up, you are drunk—that's all there is to it. I found their style of singing unique, and the alcohol seemed to evaporate with the high-frequency vibrations of their vocal cords, so they didn't get drunk easily. We followed with loud revolutionary songs, braying like donkeys, and to our surprise we drank the production team leader under the table. Such behavior was considered to be a great humiliation. At noon the next day, as we were getting ready to leave, the team leader showed up with seven or eight burly fellows, probably chosen from his production team. They were carrying several cases of beer and hard liquor, and pushing us ahead of them, we all surged into a small restaurant. Our friends were Han Chinese, but they were born and raised here and had seen this kind of battle formation many times. It was only when dishes and glasses were strewn all over the table that both sides proved their heroic mettle. The score was tied. The production team leader finally had to give up. Waving his hands and staggering, he led the crowd outside to see us off. But I had long since gone straight to the jeep and made myself horizontal.

The car passed through Dongsheng. Not really sure who we were, the mayor set up a banquet for us. Surprisingly, this small frontier town had delicacies like bird's nest soup and abalone, and we were delighted after having eaten roast mutton with our hands for many days. Who knew that, according to local custom, the mayor himself would call for three glasses of hard liquor and bring them to me on a tray, forcing me to drain each in one gulp? I weighed the situation, and of myself it could be said, "The man of little tolerance is not a gentleman," and of my opponent, "The man of no cruelty is not a hero." It was clear that if I couldn't finish the drinks, there would be no food. The friends who were with us and the local cadres all stared at me. I steeled myself for the task ahead, glanced at the sofa off to the side, and downed the three glasses one after another. Almost immediately the world began to spin and, before even picking up my chopsticks, I fell onto the sofa. When I woke up, I was just in time to grab the last mouthful of soup.

Since ancient times Chinese people have said, "If you refuse a toast, you must drink a forfeit." Drinking a toast is a form of etiquette, a kind of ceremony where you merely take a taste. Drinking a forfeit, or "drinking a fine," means getting dead drunk and making a disgraceful spectacle of yourself in public. You can still see toast drinking in Beijing opera: "The banquet is laid out . . . ," but really there is nothing on stage. Now forfeit drinking is all that's left, and this ancient disciplinary punishment has spread from government officials and businessmen all the way down to ordinary commoners, with no exceptions.

However, such drinking games are one form of the art of war—truth and deception, emptiness and fullness, offense and defense. There is a certain pleasure in them. Fortunately, guessing fists and drinking games have rallied Chinese culture. When my daughter was just learning to talk, she learned how to play drinking games from her mother and father: "One crab, eight claws, two pointy heads, just about this big." Such plain truths have been rediscovered by drinkers.

In the spring of 1983, I participated in the Zunyi Writers' Conference where I joined the crowds for a tour of the local

Dong Wine Factory. The luncheon was sumptuous, and there was a young lady at each table to keep us company as we drank. One after another, the writers drank shots with the girls. At first, the girls coyly resisted, but as time passed, they soon went on the offensive, slamming back shots, first one shot for one shot, then later matching each of the writers' shots with three of their own, until finally the men who were hoping to take advantage of them were forced to beg for mercy. Later I found out that these were specially selected workers of the distillery. They could drink liquor like water and never get drunk. The distillery had set this trap to reform lecherous men.

2

IN MY WANDERINGS OVERSEAS, alcohol has been my most loyal companion. It consoles and makes promises, it tells you that there are no difficulties that cannot be overcome, it never betrays you, and at worst it gives you a headache for a few days—just as a joke. For the first few years I lived in northern Europe, I would feel empty inside as soon as it got dark, and liquor was the only thing that kept me company during some of those long nights.

In Europe everybody has different ways of drinking. Southern Europeans primarily drink wine, and they don't guzzle it down. It is purely for the enjoyment of life—it makes the sunlight brighter and love more beautiful. Northern Europeans are ardent drinkers of hard liquor for the sake of speed so they can all the more quickly be delivered from their solitude. And, of course, there are the Russians. In the despair of their land of snow and ice they rely on vodka as a sort of club with which to beat themselves senseless. When I lived in northern Europe, that was just what I was looking for: a club to beat myself senseless with.

In 1990, I lived in Norway for three months, from autumn to winter. It was like exposing film to light—everything turned black in an instant. Fortunately, Norway produces a surplus of electricity. People are encouraged to make use of it, so lights burn in the daytime as well as at night. I lived in a student area of town, and shared a kitchen with five blond-haired, blue-eyed Norwegian men. Six cans of beer that I'd put in the refrigerator would, in a blink, be reduced to four and a half. Alcohol is controlled by the state in Norway. There are three grades of beer. The first grade has almost no alcohol at all, the second grade has only a pitiful amount, and only these two grades of beer can be bought in a supermarket. The third grade of beer, along with other types of alcohol, are sold only in state-run liquor stores. Not only is beer exorbitantly priced, but at seven every evening, with a rattle and clank, all the supermarkets lock their beer in iron cages. Even the store manager cannot help himself to a bottle. Each weekend, drinkers get up early to buy good liquor so as to get themselves half drunk at home before they go out to the bar. Otherwise, they'd go broke trying to get drunk. In Norway there are an especially large number of bootleggers, but under this liquor fascism, these guerilla warriors have no grand mission, "they just want to stay drunk."

I once watched a movie where some gorillas ate several pieces of rotten fruit that had fallen from a tree. They became unsteady, wobbling from left to right. Finally, all the gorillas fell to the ground in a deep sleep, and started to snore. If this is a scene from the source of human civilization, then the chemical reaction of fermentation still influences the way we observe and dream today.

My old friend Lichuan lives in Paris. "Old" is not actually measured by the number of years that I've known him. It's measured by the number of times we've drunk together. Each time I travel to Paris, I can't leave before I go to his house to drink. Lichuan is from Northeast China and he originally liked strong, clear liquors, but was later corrupted by French manners and fell in love with red wine. His respect for wine paraphernalia clearly shows he's been influenced by the formalism of French culture. Not only are the wine glasses well washed, he also uses paper towels to dry them one by one, not leaving even the tiniest water spot. Red wine is opened a half hour before drinking to let it breathe. Lichuan's wife is from Hangzhou and is a good cook. Getting together with a few close friends, drinking, and singing are the pleasures of living. Drinking French red wine can be a kind of a ritual: Pour it, look at the color, swish it around in the glass, let the wine swirl and breathe, smell it, take a sip, let it race through the spaces between your teeth, and finally swallow it. Is it good wine? It is good wine. After about three glasses, you are drinking voraciously and talking as if inspired about everything.

Tonight I'm drinking hard. I feel light, then stiff in the neck, head heavy, everything becomes blurry and Lichuan splits into two people. I must have drunk too much. Lichuan's voice is now nearby, now faraway, "The ancients said wine doesn't make people drunk, people make themselves drunk." I nod again and again. People need this kind of a state, a release from reality and from the pressures of life. Drunkenness is simply a fleeting interval. Sit up straight, don't lean over, and laugh foolishly with everyone else. Soon, Lichuan merges into one person again.

From northern Europe, I moved south like a migratory bird, first to the Netherlands and France, then across the Atlantic to the United States where I moved from the Midwest to warm and sunny California. Here, I gradually put aside hard liquor and fell in love with red wine. On reflection, this certainly must have something to do with the sunlight. In sunny places, people become warmer, like the personality of wine.

My first teacher in the ways of wine was Clayton Eshleman, a poet and professor of creative writing in the English department at Eastern Michigan University. He enjoyed cooking and was best at preparing French and Italian cuisine. Good food must have the assistance of a fine wine. While drinking, he would instruct me in the basics of vineyards and vintages, but the taste itself was something that cannot be passed on in words; one must learn it for oneself. After drinking myself into a state where everything was a blur, I would have the illusion that the long dining table in Clayton's house was an assembly line. He would open bottle after bottle, and the line of empty bottles would disappear at the end of the table. The Mexican masks on the wall came alive, staring ferociously and greedily at us.

Although there was a wine cellar in his basement, he drank too quickly to keep it well stocked, and the number of bottles sometimes dwindled to no more than one hundred or so. Then he'd drive all over buying wine, sometimes asking me to come along. A place we often went to was a wine shop in another small town called Royal Oak, more than an hour's drive away. The owner was Moroccan, a small man with a thievish glint in his eye. We usually arrived around noon, and he would prepare some snacks for us and open a few bottles of wine. He imported mostly obscure French wines. Clayton, in his enthusiasm and heedless of his wife Caryl's opposition, would buy four or five cases each time. Once, I also joined the fun and bought a case, planning first to leave it in Clayton's wine cellar, but then thought better of it, and carted it home to my own nest.

In 1996, I was in Taipei for a conference. One evening Li Ang, the author of *The Butcher's Wife*, took me to a bar. It was not a large place, and most of the customers were lawyers, doctors, and famous painters sitting in small groups around empty wooden crates and drinking to their hearts' content. Empty bottles formed a long line, and I noticed that all of them were well-known French wines. Drinking wine had become the new fashion in Taiwan, which was much better than having to drink XO at the dinner table. Even tastes in drinking are related to the influence of dominant cultures, and when you show off the price tag, people flock to you. Actually, French wine doesn't go well with Chinese food, especially Sichuan and Hunan cuisine where flavors are heavy and numb the tongue until there is no difference between good and bad wine.

In just a flicker, I nodded off, and quickly straightened up into a more dignified posture, pretending that nothing had happened. It was getting late, and under the supervision of Lichuan and his wife, a half-drunk friend was asked to drive me home. The streets of Paris were chilly and deserted, with only the occasional shout of a drunkard breaking the silence. At home, I staggered up the stairs and dug out my keys. No matter how hard I tried, I was unable to fit the key into the lock. Finally, I squatted down to the level of the lock and peered into the keyhole with one eye. Then with both hands in concert, I fumbled around for a good while longer before realizing that I was holding the key upside down. With a click, the door opened.

DURHAM

IN THE SPRING OF 1986, I went to London to take part in a poetry reading. Afterward, accompanied by Miss Nicola of the Great Britain-China Centre, I headed north to Durham. The East Asian Studies Department of Durham University had arranged some readings for me. While having dinner with Nicola and Don Starr, a lecturer in the East Asian Studies Department, I casually said, "It would be nice if I could stay here for a few days longer." Though it was not much more than a sigh, my two Chinese-speaking hosts took me seriously.

A year later, luggage in hand, I was looking around the Durham bus depot. It was a cold, gray day; the cathedral's bells began to ring. This was the start of my wandering days. Since March of 1987, minus the four or so months that I spent in Beijing at the end of 1988, I've been moving consistently for thirteen years. Sitting in my small apartment in Paris near the Pompidou Center, and looking back with a certain amount of schadenfreude, it seems as if that person looking around the Durham bus depot has nothing to do with me.

Don Starr picked me up. He lived in a huge, ancient country house. His wife, Jill, was a primary school teacher. They had three children: one boy and two girls. There is no great difference between winter and early spring in England. The house was like an ice cellar since it was too expensive to heat. But these people were born frozen, and the children didn't wear much, each of them like a miniature furnace giving off heat. I put on everything I could wear and still couldn't stop shivering.

Five days after I arrived, I moved into the university guesthouse that I had stayed in one year earlier. It was heated, and I revived like a plant that had wilted in the cold. A month later, Shao Fei arrived with our daughter, Tiantian. We stayed in the guesthouse for more than a month, and then moved to a row house not far from the center of town—two floors, electricity, and no phone. We were poor, but we had finally settled down.

Mr. Ma was Chinese. He had been an engineer in Australia and moved to Durham when he retired; his house was near ours. Mr. Ma had serious asthma. Every Sunday morning, he would go to Newcastle to teach English to the Chinese immigrants as a volunteer. He would take me along for the drive, drop me off in Chinatown, and pick me up again after class. Newcastle was a city in decline. Most of the shops closed on Sunday making it seem even more desolate. My job was to buy tofu, that important source of protein that has insured the continued survival of the Chinese people. He left me in Chinatown for two hours, but I always kept busy, strolling up and down the streets, stopping at the flea market, and trying my luck with the slot machines. If I lost, I would quickly retreat before putting in any of the tofu money. Mr. Ma always asked what I spent my time doing in Chinatown. Buying tofu, I would say. Just buying tofu? he would ask with a doubtful glance. Just buying tofu.

Mr. Ma eventually married an English woman named Julie, sold his house, and moved in with his new bride. They often invited us to visit. The garden at Julie's house was large and full of flowers blooming enthusiastically. Now that Mr. Ma was no longer our neighbor, he also no longer taught English—"from this time on, his majesty ceased to hold morning court"—and buying tofu became an impossible mission.

Miss Zhu taught Chinese in the East Asian Studies Department. Her father had been an air force pilot for the Kuomintang, but had died in a training accident. She had been brought up by her mother, who still lived in Hong Kong, and who still wanted to rein in her little kite that had flown so far. Miss Zhu was very kind to us. Whenever we went to the university Laundromat, we stopped by her house. She was always smiling, but her eyes had an indefinable sadness. And though she was very pretty, her emotional life hadn't been smooth. Single for many years, she used to be on good terms with a man named Kevin, but things ended in yet another breakup. She finally married an English gentleman who was much older.

Caroline was another teacher in the East Asian Studies Department. Tall, broad-shouldered, outspoken. Not long after we arrived, she drove us to a nearby beach for a picnic. This was a coal mining area—the rocks bare and black, the seawater murky. She told me that she enjoyed teaching, but didn't like doing research or writing papers. On the subject of the tunnel under the channel that was about to be constructed, she shook her head with dissatisfaction and said, "I just don't trust the French; they betrayed us in the Second World War. So how is this tunnel a good thing? The Russians can drive their tanks straight through."

Caroline later found herself a boyfriend. But just when

they were preparing for the wedding, the boyfriend was killed in a shopping center by a knife-wielding madman. After this, she became deeply depressed and finally left her job at the university. We had left Durham by that time and, when I heard about this tragedy, I remembered that picnic by the murky sea. The channel tunnel was completed, but the Russian tanks still haven't rolled in.

Don Starr was the colleague we saw most often. He came from a working-class family, and he had the simplicity and quick wit of a scholar from England's lower social class. He was a few years older than me, simultaneously balding and going gray. The pressure of teaching was very high. Every week he taught more than twenty hours, and as he was too busy to finish his doctoral thesis, he could forget about becoming a full professor. He studied Chinese history, especially the history of the Ming and Qing dynasties. One look at his Chinese name and you knew he was a historian: this Sima Lin was the younger brother of Sima Qian. He spoke deliberately and logically with an Englishman's dry wit.

Don realized that the scholarship money wasn't enough to support my family, so he found me a spot as a language teaching assistant. It was only a part-time job, but at least it was an income. I never finished high school and there I was behind the lectern at an English university. My first class every day was in the language lab, helping students smooth out their tongues. After I had taught a semester, the school went back on its word and said they wanted to pay me by the hour and not by the term. There was nothing I could do as we only had an oral agreement. Over lunch that afternoon, Don frowned and didn't utter a word. The next day he brought over a letter written in English and had me sign it. The letter, it turned out, was an ultimatum: an oral agreement was legally binding. If they did not fulfill their side of the bargain, we would see them in court.

Two days later, the school obediently turned over the full amount.

2

DURHAM IS A PEACEFUL LITTLE TOWN. A stream runs through the center. On the bridge over the stream, a homeless man always played an accordion, his yellow dog lying beside him. He was serene, concentrating on the water beneath his feet and the sound of his music. Where had he come from and where would he go? Nobody knew. From among the hurried footsteps, someone would stop and drop some coins in his empty can. They were for the poor old dog. The homeless man would nod his head and thank them on behalf of his dog.

Compared to Beijing, the streets were empty, the sky immense, and the clouds pale. When I wasn't teaching, I would wander the streets. Tiantian was only two and we sent her to a day care center. Shao Fei would drop her off at nine in the morning and pick her up at noon. The style of child care centers was different from China: in Durham, the employees let the children jump around and shout, so that after three hours, the children have burned off most of their energy and become much quieter. On the way home from the daycare center, the old English ladies who were out shopping would surround Tiantian and praise her endlessly, using all the nicest words in the English language. Tiantian was as spoiled as a world-famous movie star, and whenever she saw the old

women, she would stop and stand still until they had finished
going on about her before continuing on her way.

The most beautiful part of Durham are the lawns—great
stretches echoing each other. They are especially beautiful in
the spring, when clusters of narcissus and winter jasmine daz-
zle the eyes, blooming awake the people who have just endured winter. After dinner, Shao Fei, Tiantian, and I would go
out for a walk, strolling across the lawns and into the botanical gardens. When the birds returned to their nests, the sound
of their chatter would gradually grow fainter. The moon
would rise and the scent of the flowers would grow stronger.
Tiantian would run ahead alone, her little shadow sliding
over the lawns.

In my class there was an American student named Nate.
He was a big kid with an ingenuous smile. We arranged to
meet every Tuesday afternoon at my house, where I taught
him Chinese and he taught me English. Because we were both
pretty bad in our respective second languages, it was like
putting together two children who had just learned how to
speak. How old are you? I live in America. Do you like to read
newspapers? China is very big.

Four or five in the afternoon is the time when the English
drink tea, an unshakeable social ritual. When in Rome, you
brew tea and set out cakes. "Do people drink tea in China?"
Nate asked. I thought to myself, "What a stupid question,"
but what I said was, "In China people drink water, they sell
the tea to other countries." He laughed like a child. We were
barbarians at opposite borders of language. Later on, Nate became a literary critic, often publishing articles in American
newspapers and magazines, and he even reviewed a collection
of my poems.

I had to go to London for a reading, and Gregory Lee and

his French wife drove over from Liverpool to take us down. We had met in Beijing in 1985. He was born and raised in Liverpool, was one quarter Chinese, and understood China better than many other sinologists. While the women cooked and chatted about family life, Gregory and I headed straight for a pub.

Early the next morning we set out for London. Gregory had just bought a used white Rover, the same make of car driven by the British police, and he was feeling pleased with himself. About one hundred miles from London, two lanes of the road merged due to construction and Gregory tried to squeeze ahead of another car. He swerved over a row of plastic pylons, shattered the windshield, and almost rushed into the opposite lane of traffic. Then it began to rain and nothing could be seen through the cracked window. Gregory drove with his head stuck out the window until we made it to a garage. Tiantian said, "Let's not drive, let's walk to London." We managed to catch a train, so the accident didn't completely ruin our plans.

The poet Gu Cheng and his wife visited us at Durham. Gu Cheng was a consummate sleeper. He slept at least sixteen hours a day. After he woke up, we would talk and walk into town. When he saw street performers at work, he would beat a hasty retreat. He said he was terrified that they would ask him for money. After reading at the university, Gu Cheng gave photocopies of a picture of himself to the students. I said, "You're crazy. Why are you acting like Mao?" Xie Ye also chimed in, "You see, you see?! I said this so long ago, but he doesn't listen." On the day of his departure, Gu Cheng made *jianbing* (a kind of pancake) for us and after eating a few, I took a nap. When I woke up he was still cooking; there was a mountain of *jianbing*, enough to feed us for half a month. I yelled at him, but Gu Cheng didn't respond. He just put his hand under his hat, scratched his head, and gave me a wry smile.

On the exact day our visas expired, an immigration officer visited us and asked us when we were leaving. Whenever we crossed the border back into the U.K. from trips abroad, we were always given a thorough interrogation, just short of investigating our class background for the past three generations. The backlog of travelers behind us would start complaining. We eventually learned to wait until as many people as possible had gone through before stepping up to accept the kind attentions of the British Empire.

During childhood, we stand on tiptoes, staring into the distance to see tomorrow, always feeling we are growing too slowly, so we climb trees or other high places to see what things are going to be like. After middle age, it's all a downhill slope, and we begin looking back constantly, three sighs for every step along the way. Writing this essay about Durham, I find that compared to the vicissitudes of my life in China, almost nothing happened. I'm simply trying to make something happen when nothing did. But on second thought, isn't that a good thing? We lived in Durham for a year and three months. For me, it was a period of considerable peace before the great transitions of 1989. Actually, I think the important thing in life is not to get through it, but to experience it. Otherwise, life becomes an unread page in a book that is sent to a recycling center and pulped with other books, disappearing forever. Repeating that page would be almost impossible.

On a winter's afternoon, I'm reading on our sofa on the first floor of our place in Durham. It's cloudy and raining lightly, the wind raises the gauzy white curtains on the window. I turn on the old-fashioned floor lamp, and the radiator hisses. Upstairs Tiantian runs back and forth, her feet pounding the floor. A fly buzzes around the room, as annoying as history.

BASEBALL GAME

AT FIVE FORTY IN THE AFTERNOON, I ring the doorbell and Dan comes out to welcome me. He's just had an operation on his jaw and smiles with some effort. We drink Red Tail Ale as we talk, waiting for his wife, Betsy, to come home from work. Yesterday was Betsy's birthday. They invited me to dinner at an Italian restaurant where they mentioned they had two extra tickets to a baseball game and urged me to go with them. I declined but then reconsidered.

Dan is two years younger than me. He is a building contractor and a poet. We live in the same town, and we both work Tuesday evenings at a poetry workshop in Sacramento where he is one of the coordinators. Not long after we met, we became good friends.

The telephone rings. It is Betsy. She works for the state government in Sacramento and can't make it home in time, so she arranges to meet us at the Rio City Café near the baseball stadium. The ale has higher alcohol content than regular beer, and I drink mine too quickly. Fortunately, Dan drives. We hit the road at six. Not long ago at the university, Dan tells me, he heard a speech where the speaker thoroughly denied the theory of evolution. The speaker believed that most books written today were full of nonsense, like the idea that humans were the highest form of animal life. Actually, the speaker said, people are no higher than germs, for even people's enormous power over life and death is still decided by them. Dan thinks I would appreciate an idea as heterodox as this. I close my eyes and drift off, thinking I am indeed no better than a germ, for a germ wouldn't feel dizzy after a single bottle of beer.

Our town is only about a twenty-minute drive to Sacramento. The stadium is downtown, right next to an old bridge that crosses the Sacramento River. Dan drives circles around Old Town but can't find a place to park, so we have to drive across the bridge and park in the temporary parking lot outside the stadium. Then we walk back across the bridge into town. The river is wide and its waters, parted by the bridge's supports, spin in numerous eddies. On the bridge's narrow sidewalk we walk right into a wave of people who jostle past us, evidently on their way to the baseball game.

The Rio City Café is by the river in a renovated train station. The ceiling is high, and six silver fans turn slowly, purely for show as the place has central air. The bar is crowded with people, probably all of them here to have a drink before the game. We find Betsy and their friend Old Tom. Old Tom is a lawyer who works in the statehouse. His face glows with health. White hair, white beard, the ends of his mustache curl up. He is wearing a baseball cap that reads "1987 Pennant Game" above a picture of an old American fellow with a curly mustache in a stovepipe hat who looks just like him.

Dan orders a cocktail. Still in a daze, I follow him and order a beer, then listen to Old Tom talk about a low-income family housing project. The more I drink, the dizzier I feel. I move up against the bar in search of something to lean against.

At exactly seven o'clock, I cross the old bridge with them, trying to keep my steps as steady as possible. Tom tells me about the history of the bridge and the days of the gold rush. He moved here twenty-five years ago from Baltimore, where he was born and raised. Before he became a lawyer he piloted a steamer and coached football in the Navy.

The stadium's fourteen thousand seats are all filled. There are even people on the lawn opposite the bleachers. The loudspeakers blare, the game begins. Dan goes to buy a beer and asks if I want another glass. I still have trouble standing and can only manage to shake my hand no.

We finally sit down. I am between Dan and Old Tom, holding a tub of popcorn. Today the River Cats are playing the Las Vegas Stars. Old Tom, Dan, and Betsy have played baseball since they were children. I know nothing about baseball. In primary school I played soccer and in high school I played basketball, and was awful at both. I spent a lot of time on the bench. Sometimes, though, they let me on the court, and once, when no one was guarding me, I took three steps and shot, narrowly missing the wrong hoop.

Dan and Tom take turns explaining the rules of the game and only deepen my confusion. For example, why does the guy with the bat just watch the ball fly back and forth without taking a swing? Dan says the coaches gestures are secret signals that sometimes tells the batter when to swing. In America, not being a sports fan is seen as wasting your life.

Dan points out that I've eaten almost the entire tub of popcorn.

A swallow flies low overhead. It takes at most ten seconds for it to fly over the field and the bleachers. This kind of human assembly must leave a strange impression on a swallow.

At eight ten the score is zero-zero. The growing glare of the setting sun reflecting off the glass of a building is much brighter than the lights shining down on the field. Someone dressed as a stuffed toy bear paces along the edge of the field, then chases its tail in a circle, then, along with a couple of girls, shoots candy up into the stands with a slingshot. Vendors selling popcorn, peanuts, and cotton candy weave in and out among the spectators, crying their wares.

"No wonder there are so many fat Americans," I say.

"The key reason is that lifestyles have changed," Tom explains. "Before, during my father's generation, most people engaged in physical labor and ate the same types of food with no problems. Nowadays we all sit at desks, using our brains not our brawn."

At nine o'clock it's still zero-zero. The loudspeakers broadcast the song "YMCA". The entire audience sings along, everyone stretching their arms into letters. Dan buys a box of Cracker Jacks. The surprise inside is just a few sheets of paper. When opened, it reveals Jack's words of wisdom: "Your fingernails are made of the same stuff as a bull's horns."

DEATH VALLEY

IN 1849, THIRTY GOLD MINERS seeking a shortcut got lost in the desert. One of the eighteen survivors named the place of their wanderings Death Valley.

Occupying more than three million acres, Death Valley is the largest national park in America. We went there over Thanksgiving with Old Li and his family. Old Li is from Shandong, grew up in Shanghai, and was sent to a production team in the Northeast to be reeducated. You can tell at a glance that he's a Northeasterner, dark and strong. He doesn't often speak the gentle Wu dialect of Shanghai in public. From the point of view of sound construction, this makes sense, as how could a horn make the sounds of a flute or strings? He recently received a Ph.D. in ecology and was staying in California to do some post-doctoral work. An expert on environmental protection, he had also studied ore dressing. We couldn't have asked for a better tour guide. A month before the trip he had already begun to prepare—assembling information, collecting maps, reserving rooms, and renting cars.

There were a total of ten of us on this trip. I was driving a Camry and Old Li lead the way in his rented Volvo. "Volvo" in Latin means "I turn," but the Chinese phrase, *fuhao* ("rich and powerful man"), is almost certainly a translation by some Hong Kong marketing guru. There was an article in the *New York Times* recently that said the titles of foreign movies in Hong Kong were almost always translated into a four-character phrase about some key aspect of the story. So, in this way the Chinese translation of "I turn" as "rich and powerful man" makes sense since only a rich and powerful man deserves to sit behind one of these "turning" wheels.

Following Old Li's itinerary, we stopped for a break at the small town of Visalia. At the beginning of the century, this town thrived as a farming and ranching community. But now, seeing the current state of decline, this seemed like a magnificent rumor. The houses looked like they were made of cheese and were about to melt and become one with the earth. We picnicked on the lawn in the middle of town. The people who passed by us, mostly the homeless, behaved suspiciously. The sun was bright and pleasant. As uninvited guests, we brought an unexpected romantic moment to this dying little town.

The children were all gathered together in the "rich and powerful man," where they were listening to the songs of Fan Xiaoxuan and Zhou Huajian. Those of us following behind—now closely, now at a distance—were listening to a piano performance by Horowitz in Moscow. The only connection between the two generations was a walkie-talkie. Even if you shouted into it at the top of your lungs, there was still no response from the other side. Only when we caught up to them, drove alongside, rolled down our windows, and shouted and gesticulated wildly did the walkie-talkies finally tune in and produce any sound: "Yam, Yam, this is Potato, come in Yam. . . ."

By the time we got to Baker, it was already dark. The world's largest thermometer stood in the center of town, and the highest temperature on record was 134 degrees. Baker was established fifty years ago as the gate to Death Valley.

We checked into the Bun Boy Motel, lugging our sleeping bags, pots, bowls, ladles, and plates into two hotel rooms, one for each gender. After cleaning up, we all went to a nearby restaurant called the Mad Greek. The Mad Greek was not in the least bit crazy, in fact both the host and the patrons looked dull and listless. But if the temperature ever did rise to 134 degrees, I imagine everyone would go mad. The Mad Greek had vulgar, fast food restaurant décor and a strong flavor of forced cheerfulness. Autographed photos of Hollywood movie stars hung on the walls.

At six thirty the next morning, we cooked some instant noodles in the rice cooker and roused the kids, who lined up to use the bathroom. I had drunk enough grain spirits with Old Li before going to bed that there was pain in the very center of my brain. Setting out from Baker, we entered Death Valley; Shao Fei drove and I dozed. I can only remember that the road was very narrow but surrounded by wide-open spaces, like an old dream. I didn't wake up until we reached Zabriskie Point. We got out and climbed. A flock of mountains swelled before us, from bluish grays to yellowish ochre, unfolding like a symphony. Under Old Li's direction, the volcanoes erupted, the earth's crust shifted, wrinkling up into mountains or making cofferdams that filled with lakes, then the lake waters evaporated leaving salt flats, millions of years passing with a wave of his hands.

In the summer, the surface temperature reaches 180 degrees. Surprisingly, some plants thrive here. One has ashy white leaves that move like small bells in the wind, and when you touch them, they disappear like smoke, crumbling like ashes. Old Li explained that this kind of plant has an instinct for self-preservation. During the long dry season it shuts down completely, allowing its leaves and branches to dry out all the way, but it conserves the last necessary bit of water in its roots, awaiting the arrival of the rainy season. This is a kind of internal spiritual discipline of a life that will procreate until the end of heaven and earth.

We reached Twenty Mule Team Canyon. In 1873, a man named Coleman discovered borax deposits there and built a wagon to haul out the ore with twenty mules. We entered the mountains along a ravine, and ventured into a great fold in the earth. These low, yellow mountains were round and bare, the soil was soft and light, a little like the loess plains of northern Shaanxi. I suddenly felt like singing a northern Shaanxi folk song, and spent some time doing breathing warm-ups, but didn't sing out loud.

The Devil's Golf Course is a strange land of alkali and crushed stones left behind after the lakes had evaporated. It is uneven with small holes everywhere. Indeed, only a devil could play golf in such a place. They say that in the summer you can hear the salt crystals expand.

Badwater is 282 feet below sea level. The "bad water" is actually a pool formed by a gushing spring with high levels of chlorine, sodium, and sulfur, but it contains no poisons. The pool is surrounded by vast stretches of white salt flats, and further out, a ring of mountains. Walking on the salt flats was like walking on the snow and ice of another planet. The sky grew cloudy, and a bluish mist swept over us. We were like a school of fish moving through some great, prehistoric sea.

At three in the afternoon, we picnicked in the desert. When we had eaten and drunk our fill, the boys played football with an empty soda bottle, tossing it back and forth. Tiantian and Old Li's daughter rolled down the hills of sand, screaming with delight. Shao Fei and I took a walk. It was a middle-aged afternoon, sunlight sprinkled down from among the clouds. There were few signs of life around us save for some ferns, flies, and a team of enormous ants on the march.

The sky darkened as we drove out of Death Valley. We made the sharp turns going down the mountain listening to Slavonic Dance No. 5. The music made everyone a bit agitated. Had Dvořák anticipated such an effect?

We spent the night at Lone Pine. Dawn the next day, light rain.

IV

SHIFU

THE TERM OF ADDRESS SHIFU ("master" or "teacher") came into widespread use in the early 1980s, serving as a transition between "comrade," and "Mr." or "Miss." In the struggle between the two classes, this term was seriously worn down, and its original connotations of seniority, age, skill, talent, and even its inherent sense of gender all disappeared.

I was in the construction business for eleven years, five years as a concrete mixer and six years as an ironworker, and I never attained Shifu status. I worked long enough to become Shifu, but I was never proficient enough in either job. If you remain a second-class worker and never get a raise, why would anyone ever call you Shifu? But a number of people were Shifu to me. In fact, with the exception of my students, almost everyone is my Shifu.

In March of 1969, I reported for duty at the Beijing Sixth Construction Company, packed myself and my luggage into a truck, and was taken to the worksite in Wei County, Hebei Province. Our job was simple and clear: blast open a mountain and build a power plant in the hole.

My first Shifu was Xiang Guilin, a level six carpenter who managed a group of students and local workers in handling odd jobs on the site. Xiang Shifu was from Hebei, and right away you could tell he was a simple, honest person. He didn't speak much, but he was always grinning, displaying all the good-natured wrinkles on his face. He had worked in a mine before and got black lung, which resulted in a fearsome cough. When we school graduates arrived to work, we always formed a clump to talk. But if Xiang Shifu walked by, we all started to work without a single word from him.

Fat Zhang, a demoted accountant, and Donkey lived with Xiang Shifu. Every evening at political study, the whole crew squeezed into their little room where we smoked and dozed. The student workers would become more energetic as we took turns reading books and newspapers in loud, clear voices. Xiang Shifu couldn't read and he was a bit confused about the concepts of Marxism. With his two thick hands, he would roll a fat "cannon" cigarette, light it up, and instantly, a thick fog obscured his face.

Donkey was my classmate in junior high school. He was quite tall, wore thick glasses, and walked with a ridiculous waddle. How could you avoid being noticed during the Cultural Revolution with posture like that? He always carried around a Hongmei brand transistor radio. One day, a large-character poster was taped up stating that he was secretly listening to American music. When Xiang Shifu found out, he hopped around cursing him. We had never seen him so angry. Someone was sent to the site to look into the matter, but he gave them his assurance, "Nothing like this has ever happened." Donkey was off the hook.

Several months later, we were officially assigned to work groups. I was assigned to the concrete team. I often saw Xiang Shifu at the site laying line with Donkey. While I dug a trench, he'd squat and smoke at its edge, the open sky behind him. Then he'd start coughing violently. Two years later, while talking in the dormitory, I learned that Xiang Shifu had died of lung cancer. I couldn't keep myself from breaking down into loud sobs, which puzzled all the other Shifu who were there. Death at the work site is like a gust of wind—it leaves no trace.

Meng Qingjun was from Shandong. He was small and dark-skinned, with bulging eyes and a dirty mouth. He was almost fifty, but the other Shifu all called him Little Meng. Liu Shifu, the head of our group, always made fun of him. Just after Liberation, Little Meng traveled from Shandong to Beijing. It was his first time on a train. Right after buying his ticket, the train left the station without him. He stood on the platform pointing at it and shouting a torrent of curses: "Train! I'm going to fuck your grandmother!" When he finally got to Beijing, he wanted to send a package back home and asked someone whether it was faster to mail things by train or by wire. He was told the wire service was faster, so he climbed a telegraph pole, tied his package to a wire, and the next day, sure enough, it was gone.

At the Wei County site, Little Meng was one of the safety personnel in the hole, but he was later transferred to my work group. One day while we were working the night shift, carrying the steel supports we had just taken apart to the other slope of the mountain, Little Meng suddenly got angry, spat, threw his gloves on the ground, and swore, "Shit! These goddamned blind directors are just wasting our time!" He squatted down on the ground and went on strike. The group leader had to swallow his anger and keep working around him. This situation was like one in the world of politics when a senior statesman has a few sharp words for His Majesty, who must listen patiently.

Not long thereafter, we were transferred to the East Is Red oil refinery in a distant suburb of Beijing, and Little Meng formally became my Shifu. We both wore tall plastic boots all day long, dragging around concrete mixers and trudging through the freshly poured cement. It was like a race with no finish line and the referee was death, who was waiting to see which of us would be the first to use up his life in this profession. Meng Shifu had a fairly high estimation of my labor: "He's not afraid to get dirty, he's just afraid to get tired." After work, I would read late into the evening, and every morning he would shout at me, "You stay up at night like a cat, and the next morning you're like a dead rat!" Now I shout the same thing to my daughter.

After we had put up a number of buildings, our dormitory was renovated and we moved from a huge work shed that housed more than one hundred people to an undecorated, plastered building. Meng Shifu, another man, and I shared a room. It was pure luxury. At site meetings, the directors would come by shouting and pounding on each door as they passed. I would lock the door from the inside and hide in our room to read; Meng Shifu would roll his goldfish eyes, but he always covered for me.

His speech could be acerbic. One summer day during our noon break, some of my friends and I went to swim at the ravine. We were each wearing swimming trunks and wrapped ourselves in rubber raincoats. Meng Shifu looked down on this. Laughing, he said in his thick Shandong accent, "Why so shy? Next time why don't you wear a little less? Maybe just a condom."

Meng Shifu managed to get his hands on a heap of camel wool yarn from Inner Mongolia and wanted to knit himself a pair of pants. He first asked some female workers for some knitting tips before returning home to mull over each point in his mind. Then each night while I read or wrote, Meng Shifu would put on his reading glasses and knit, stitch by stitch, to the sound of the water pot hissing on the stove. Beginning in autumn, he knitted into spring, winter passing along with the old man's chance to wear his wool pants. Even worse, when the legs of the pants were half done, he ran out of yarn. And if you looked carefully, you could see the pants were so thick and stiff that if you stood them up on the ground, they would stay standing, like old-fashioned armor.

In 1974, I was transferred to an ironworkers' group in Work Zone Three, where I hammered iron with Yan Shifu. I have forgotten Yan Shifu's real name. He was short and skinny, the smallest size work uniform was still visibly too large for him. His beat-up hat was marked with sweat stains, its brim flopping down over his face. He was a man of few words; sometimes he mumbled phrases that nobody could make out. The conversations between the two of us, Shifu and apprentice, took place for the most part at the anvil. When his little hammer started clanging away, my fourteen-pound sledge would follow soon after, light and heavy, quick and slow, the sounds rising and falling. When the metal darkened and ceased to give off sparks, and I was drenched with sweat and stars danced before my eyes, this was the moment the conversation between the two hammers was happiest. As soon as his little hammer stopped, Yan Shifu would wave his hand for me to go back to the dormitory. He was aware of my bad habit of reading. While I read he'd be busy quenching, polishing, or straightening up the blast furnace. Sometimes I'd forget about work while reading, and Yan Shifu would come to my dormitory and call out, "Little Zhao!" then turn and leave.

Soon I got a fellow apprentice. Little Wang had originally been a frame worker, but had fallen from a ladder and hurt his back. He was big and broad-shouldered and much stronger than me. The conversation between two big hammers and one small hammer was really very stirring. Little Wang kept hoping to switch his big hammer for a little one, and would use his hammering to discuss it with Yan Shifu. His big hammer would thump and thump, always asking, "When can I be a Shifu?" And the little hammer would answer, "Never!"

Quenching is the key to working iron. Sometimes, when Yan Shifu was gone, Little Wang took charge of the small hammer. One time, the blade of a newly repaired pick that wasn't successfully quenched cracked. Little Wang cursed Yan Shifu behind his back for being too cautious. Not only was the relationship between Shifu and apprentice one of power, it also contained emotional elements. Plus the transmission of the skill wasn't easy. Yan Shifu tried to teach me several times, but I wasn't interested. He'd turn and stalk off unhappily, probably muttering something like this to himself: "Reading books . . . hmpf . . . What's the fucking use of reading books? Don't take the time to learn a skill, then you might as well go drink the northwest wind. . . ."

MUSTARD

I

A CERTAIN RICH MAN NAMED Mr. Zheng was once register-
ing at an American casino and, when asked his name, shook
his head as if to say, "I don't understand." So the people
in the casino called him Jim, a name he transliterated back
into Chinese as a sort of condiment with character: *jiemo*
("mustard").

That Mustard and I became friends at all must have been
arranged by the gods, as it is beyond human comprehension.
We had absolutely nothing in common. He was a businessman, I wrote poems; he threw money around like it was dirt,
my pockets were always empty; he was the king of his own
mountain, while I was busy wandering the world; he was a
high ranking police officer who had retired with honor, and
me, well, I was a fugitive. Who would have thought that four
years ago we would both move to a town so small it's hard to
find it on a map.

Mustard was from northeast China. Skinny, not very tall,
crew cut, a pair of cheerful, protruding ears. He was born in a
village on the Jiaodong Peninsula in Shandong, and when he
was eight years old, he and his grandfather went to the
Northeast to search for his father, a forester. His childhood

was spent in a poverty that was forever etched in his memory. In his own words: "Before I was fifteen, I didn't even have long underwear despite the freezing cold." After finishing junior high school, he stayed in the timberland and worked as a boiler man on a small train. His classification was that of second-level worker, and he got five dollars less than a first-level worker, which disgruntled him. One day, he got up early, went to work, and said that he was too sick to do anything. The Shifu shook his head, not knowing what to do with him, and made the second engineer stoke the boiler. Mustard lay down and slept on the platform between the head of the train and the coal car. While passing over a bridge, the train jumped the rails, and the logs loaded on the train slid instantly toward the front car, smashing the heads of the two Shifu inside. From his dreams, he plunged directly into an icy river. He pulled himself out and staggered the forty li back to the depot to report what had happened. It was only when he made it back to the field office that he discovered his right arm was broken.

After this event, he enlisted in the army. His father had built a large wardrobe cabinet for the company commander, and Mustard was given the cushy job of driving the senior officer. At the end of the '70s, he tested into a school for political science and law, and after graduating he worked for the Public Security Bureau. In the jargon of the Mainland, he and I were considered to be "a perfect professional match," and the people he spied on were none other than people like me. Things I said may have gotten him promotions and raises. Even today his protruding ears still move like radar dishes, but this town is too quiet and his professional skills are deteriorating.

Mustard has a photographic memory for numbers, but he refuses to learn English. When the need arises, he uses gestures and spits out a few isolated English words. Last year he went with me to buy a used car. The owner was selling it for five thousand dollars, but Mustard impatiently held out four fingers, his mouth following up with, "Four dollar!" boldly making an offer that was less than one tenth of one percent of the asking price. The car seller almost flew into a rage.

One time he went to an ATM to get money. He deftly swiped his card and—tap, tap, tap—entered "two hundred" for the amount; but to his surprise, the machine spit out a pile of stamps. Mustard doesn't write many letters, so these two hundred dollars worth of postage stamps will probably last him a lifetime.

It is not entirely correct for me to say that Mustard cannot speak English. When it comes to the casino jargon—from amounts of money, to gambling regulations, to suits, ranks, and groupings of cards—there's nothing he doesn't understand. He also has an especially wide range of gestures—depression, vacillation, anger, curses—which are universally understood. This is especially true of his victorious slapping of the table that always produces a special dread in the losers. There was even a period of time when Mustard worked a daily shift in a casino. I once went with him to a casino on a nearby Indian reservation. As soon as we opened the door, he was greeted by a number of people. Mustard puffed out his chest, sucked in his stomach, waved his hands, and smiled. Whenever he sat down at a card table, the dealers were especially deferential to him. He had his own account at the casino and ate and drank for free. With a sort of aristocratic style, his facial expression never changed when he lost. I saw him lose eight hundred dollars with the wave of a hand; afterward he earnestly informed me, "Gambling is really no different from business: If you are afraid to lose, you will never win."

Last spring, he won five hundred dollars at a casino on top of the seven hundred dollars he had in his pocket. When he returned to our town, he realized he couldn't just leave it at that, so he went right past his own house, rented a car, and headed for Reno. The road winds through the mountains for most of the way and it began to snow. Mustard was supposed to put on tire chains, but as soon as he heard they cost sixty dollars, he immediately asked for his money back, saying "No!" to the worker, slapping his own chest, and sticking out his thumb, the meaning of which was clear: I drive very well on my own and do not need chains. They returned his money, but he didn't get far before a police car pulled him over. The policeman ignored his gestures, smacked him with an eighty-dollar traffic ticket, and called a tow truck. The driver of the tow truck hoisted up both car and driver, fastening the car to the bed of the truck. In all his time in the U.S., Mustard had never enjoyed such glory. High above the other cars, his view was wide-open. With one police car leading the way and another behind, it really felt like a procession for a head of state. Unfortunately, before the tow truck drove very far, it stopped in front of a shop. In addition to paying for the tow, Mustard also had to buy some chains, and, on top of that, he had to pay to have them put on. Then, when he got to Reno, he had to spend more money to have someone remove the luckless chains. Before even entering the casino, he'd already been shorn of two hundred dollars, and Dame Fortune would keep her back turned on him. Soon he was down to nine dollars and didn't have enough money to have someone put the chains back on his tires. Mustard pointed to the wrinkled bills with his finger, patted his pockets, and spread out his hands. Casino workers have seen it all, and somehow they helped him put the chains back on the tires. But this nine-dollar job had some problems. When the rental company inspected the car, they discovered the chains had chipped the body paint. You didn't buy insurance? No cash? That's easy enough to fix. A female employee escorted him to the bank where he withdrew the money. But five hundred dollars wasn't enough. They also sent him a bill for twelve hundred dollars to cover the repairs. As an even greater stroke of ill luck, Mustard was put on the company's permanent blacklist.

I began hanging out with Mustard in the summer of 1997. We mostly swapped gambling stories, but at some point I was shocked to find out that he also enjoyed poetry. After borrowing a collection of my poems, he would sometimes recite lines at random, startling me, making me think he had overheard my secret voice. Somehow a former policeman and a current counterrevolutionary had found a shared spiritual sympathy.

As I write this, the telephone rings. It is Mustard. We haven't been in touch for more than six months. I heard that he'd been doing business in China but that he had bungled it. Now he must keep up a household for his green card, and pay the numerous and exorbitant American taxes. He and his wife were forced to get work in a Chinese restaurant. I invited him over, and he appeared as soon as the words were out of my mouth. His hand had a knife wound on it that had been hastily bandaged. Rolling up his sleeves, he exposed arms that were covered with blister scars—but he was even more spirited than before. Mustard did a little bit of everything in the restaurant kitchen—wash dishes, man the fryer, and even cook for weddings and funerals. He worked twelve-hour days, could eat and drink whatever he wanted, and never had any trouble falling asleep at night.

At around noon, I took him to a Chinese restaurant downtown for a simple lunch. Mustard falls in love with whatever job he's currently doing. When he went into the food service industry, he learned all there was to know about the healthiest dishes, various cooking processes, and what restaurants made the most money. For him, coming to the U.S. was the biggest mistake of his life, but there was nothing to be done about it. Now neither his wife nor his children wanted to go back. As for the future, he planned to keep working, get some money together, buy his own restaurant, and stage a comeback.

"Everyone in politics is a thug and everyone in business is a thief. . . . With the exception of smuggling drugs, what the hell haven't I done? What kind of person haven't I seen? Having come this far, I can finally see that enjoying life is the most important thing of all." As he said this, his eyes reddened, and he turned his head to the window. There was construction going on outside and the window was covered with green canvas.

Mustard told me that he had gone straight and stopped gambling. Sometimes, late at night, he drives the restaurant's illegal-immigrant workers to a casino, charging five dollars a person for the ride, and then he sleeps in the car. Sometimes he goes in with them to take a look around and give them suggestions. And once, after they won, they asked him if he'd ever gambled. He shook his head and walked away.

"Someone the country's discharged / passes through a stifling-hot midday nap / reaches a beach, dives down deep," he said, quoting one of my poems, and then sighed, "I was fifteen before I even wore long underwear. What am I afraid of?"

2

AFTER MORE THAN A YEAR of staggering around overseas, I returned to our small town. I gave Mustard a call and he came right over. During this time, his life had undergone yet another dramatic change. It seems it won't be easy for the author to keep up with his subject's pace in this particular piece of nonfiction.

Mustard had aged visibly, gray hairs covered his head. When he spoke of something that moved him, his little eyes would start to blink and fill with tears. He now believed in the Lord. Every Friday evening, he studied the Bible with other church members. On Sundays, he went to church and raised his voice in song.

Ever since Mustard moved to the U.S. in 1995, his business in China has gradually collapsed. In 1997, Viagra was born into the world. He immediately understood the significance this revolutionary medicine would have for reinvigorating China, so he borrowed money from friends, hid some here, stashed some there, and managed to bring Viagra to China—a redemption for his long suffering countrymen. "Of course," he said with a tight smirk, "I also made a little money in the process."

In the fall of 1998, he gathered all his money, including his Viagra profits, accumulated more debt with friends and family, took out a bank loan, and raised the flag on yet another campaign. This would be the greatest venture of Mustard's career, everything resting on its success or failure. If it succeeded, he would return to the U.S. and live comfortably with his wife. With decades of experience, he decided to lay this final wager: open a casino (every gamblers' dream) in China.

He led his mighty forces into a county in the Yantai area of Shandong, first initiating a collaboration with the local police and underworld figures, then bringing in a renowned dealer from a Macao casino. When the dealer arrived to show off his skills, Mustard finally understood where all his gambling money had gone. "It was all a goddamned scam," he told me. The dealer told Mustard that he should act fast and get out quick because the casino would not last ten days.

The casino opened. The people of Jiaodong are the kind of gamblers that a casino owner is happiest to see—hot tempered and impulsive. The more impatient they become, the faster they lose their money. And the money poured in every day. Mustard was very pleased with himself. After ten days, he could not have stopped if he'd wanted to. Four or five more days passed. Then the officials and gangs stole back almost everything he had.

With his police background, Mustard had sensed something was amiss. On the fateful morning, he instructed his bodyguards to quietly rent two cars, and he and the dealer raced out of danger. First he went to Qingdao to lay low until things settled down. Then he spent some money to open up some channels to get his friends out of trouble one by one. He went with some friends to talk to the local underworld bosses and left with a loose front tooth and a black eye. Keeping his anger in check, he returned to his hometown, disbanded his forces, and nursed his wounds at his father-in-law's house for a few days. By the time he flew back to the U.S., he only had half of one dollar RMB.

"Look," he said grinning, wiggling his front tooth. Indeed, the tooth stood out of the crowd. I was afraid that he was going to pull it out.

So it seemed Mustard's cupboard was again bare. His wife

found a part-time job in a restaurant, while he stayed at home unemployed and dejected. He eventually decided to go out incognito and make some inquiries to test the waters. He came from a poor background, was a very adept worker, and could learn any skill quickly. He started off cleaning houses and painting, then moved on to trimming trees. His boss would lift him up in the giant scoop of a bulldozer with a safety rope tied around his waist. It was a like a special-effects shot in a kung fu movie: floating through the forest with a chainsaw in hand.

He got a job in a restaurant. The boss asked him, Do you have any experience as a fry cook? Yes. How long have you worked? Five years. Okay, your starting salary is thirteen hundred dollars. To save on personnel costs, the fryer, the refrigerator, and the dishwasher were arranged in a ring, leaving just enough space in the center for one person. At the same time, Mustard fried chicken wings with his left hand, flipped things with a spatula in his right, watched the sweet-and-sour pork sauce, and used his knees to control the switch to the stove's vent. He also had to keep one eye on the dishes that piled up and his two radar-dish ears pricked up, alert for the distant calls of the boss or the waiters.

Within three years' time, he probably worked in thirty different restaurants. He had a quick temper and his bosses were conniving. Mustard would inevitably end up slapping the table indignantly, rising to his feet, and settling up his pay before leaving.

Under the influence of her boss's wife, Mustard's wife had become a Christian. He muddled along after her and was baptized. At church activities, he was generally exhausted from work and often nodded off. Other members of the congregation said that he was sleeping in God's arms. "Eh, sleeping in

God's arms. Not bad," he said with a strange kind of smile. He hated dogma, liked enlightened ministers, and character-ized himself as a defective Christian. This was just the oppo-site of his philosophy when he was a businessman and all the damaged and substandard products were marked as having passed inspection.

Later he moved to a Japanese restaurant where he contin-ued working the wok. When he heard that the sushi chef made three thousand dollars a month in wages and tips, all in cash, he was inspired to change his trade. He tried to talk to the Japanese sushi chef, but they had no common language. Fortunately, someone who knows Japanese can read a good number of Chinese characters, so they communicated with writing and gestures (Mustard still had an especially large number of gestures). As they began to communicate more, the Japanese sushi chef realized that Mustard wanted to give him five hundred dollars a month for half a year to secretly teach him the art of making sushi. "No." The Japanese sushi chef shook his head. "Yes." Mustard turned and left. On pay-day, he forced five hundred dollars into the hands of the sushi chef. Six months later, he moved to a new establishment as a sushi chef.

One evening Mustard treated three of us—our friend Li Tuo, me, and my daughter—to dinner at his new restaurant. We drove into Walnut Creek, the neon lights of the restaurant flashed on. Mustard stood grinning behind the sushi bar, dressed in a blue Japanese outfit with a sharp knife in hand. The boss was Taiwanese and he served us some sake. Mustard talked with us as he worked. During a break from his knife-play, he told us that his nickname was a bad influence, for now he dealt with wasabi mustard all day long. His sushi skills were formidable, and he had even learned a few new phrases of English such as, "How many California rolls would you like?"

A few days later, someone reported a series of violations to the police. The restaurant was soon shut down. So Mustard decided to open his own sushi restaurant. He itemized the various possibilities on his outstretched fingers—the prospects were impressive. I had almost forgotten that he used to be a boss himself. Mustard searched around town, finally settling on a former Mexican restaurant that was ideal in every way, except for the crows. It was a spot in town where the crows were thickest, especially around sunset, filling the air with their disheartening cawing. Crow excrement is extremely corrosive. If it falls on your car and you don't scrape it off right away, it can leave permanent marks. This was sure to affect business.

Last weekend I invited Mustard over for dinner. He seemed rather distracted and, right after he arrived, said he needed to check on something. He didn't return for quite a while. With his policeman's powers of observation, he made a precise record: 6:10, crows come in from all directions; 6:20, they start settling onto tree branches; 6:40, they stop moving. His explanation was that the crows first held a meeting, then slept. But the problem was whether or not the crows still shat while they slept. He still wasn't sure. Mustard ate dinner anxiously, worried about the crows.

THE ECCENTRIC JIAKAI

WHEN MY YOUNGER BROTHER visited me in Paris, Jiakai had him bring me ten exquisite fish of various sizes, each made of enamel inlaid with gold thread. These fish moved their heads, wiggled their tails, and would have been able to swim in water if only they had been lighter. The fish were made at his wife's factory.

In the early 1970s, I got to know the literary critic Dazhong through a high school friend. He taught in a vocational high school, spoke eloquently, and smoked cigars. He was crammed full of knowledge, which floated into the air with the smoke. He was a born critic, but unfortunately in those years there were no books to review. He had to make due disguising model plays like *The Harbor* and revolutionary films like *Spring Bud* in the garb of nineteenth-century Russian literary theories that he had painstakingly researched. Who would have thought that even these reviews would meet the same fate as underground literature? There simply was no place to publish anything, so he hid his writing.

At that time Dazhong once revealed that one of his classmates in the vocational school, Jiakai, liked my poetry. One night, when I lay in bed reading, there was a knock at the door. Someone bustled up to the foot of my bed, reeking of alcohol, with flecks of saliva flying from his mouth as he spoke. I was startled, but as I listened, I realized he was heaping praise upon my poetry, saying I was even greater than the contemporary poet he worshipped the most, Wu Sanyuan (Who on earth was Wu Sanyuan?). I was young then and not good at dealing with praise, which in this instance was making me dizzy. Before I had time to gather my wits, he vanished as abruptly as he had arrived.

That was my first meeting with Jiakai. Thirty years have passed in a flash. He is five or six years older than me, so he must be nearly sixty now. I still remember him in his youth: stocky build, his hair a mess, the frames of his glasses wrapped in tape. When he laughed, his mouth frowned as if the laughter might turn into sobs at any moment. His father died a horrible death during the Cultural Revolution. When he spoke of this, he stared straight ahead, his face turning murderous. He's been an alcoholic for as long as I've known him, relieving his sorrow with drink after drink then suddenly bursting into tears. He referred to "drinking wine" as "eating wine." After he had eaten himself drunk, he could do anything short of flying. Once, after gambling, he goose stepped barefoot down Wangfujing Avenue, carrying his shoes and socks on his head.

Jiakai lived in Shichahai, not far from my house, in a tiny room on the second floor of a dilapidated little building squeezed between the luxurious residences of two high-ranking officials who worked for the Central Athletics Committee. Through the crack in his door, you could spy on the girl who lived in the next room. Jiakai worked as a technician for the Beijing Number Two Machine Tool Plant and lingered on the sick list collecting worker's insurance. He loved drink like life itself and eventually ended up selling off his possessions to pay for alcohol, until finally, there were no longer even any chairs. All that remained were a bed, a table, a pot, and a bowl.

We once had a few drinks at a place near Di'anmen. At the next table sat two men and a woman, young and wholesome. It was immediately clear that they were the children of cadres. We began talking with them. They were quite congenial and soon we were sitting and drinking together. Not yet in the mood to end the evening, Jiakai invited them back to his house. As soon as he pushed open the door to his place, he called out loudly, "In front of me lives the official Li Qingchuan, in the back is Chen Buxue, and here in the middle is my humble abode." These three, all from wealthy and powerful families, were stunned by the utter poverty of his "humble abode." They looked at each other and began to laugh. After the three of them were seated on his table, he realized that there was no tea to serve the guests and no glasses to drink from. The host and I stood to the side, leaning against the wall as we talked late into the night. Isn't this exactly what Liu Yuxi meant in his "Inscription for a Humble Room" when he ended with Confucius's question: "What crudeness is here?"

One morning I went to see him. He was not wearing a shirt and just sat on the bed doing nothing. I invited him to go out for a walk, but he stubbornly refused. Why? He pointed at the wire clothes rack in the middle of the room where a worn, dripping-wet blue uniform hung. He had no other clothes. There was nothing to do but keep him company. (In those days people were more patient.) Fortunately, it was a hot day so we waited as the water quickly evaporated, wisp by invisible wisp. At about noon, he put on the damp clothes and we went out.

Jiakai was angry at the world and its ways, and his head was full of muddled thoughts. Especially after he had eaten some liquor, one ridiculous theory after another poured out. I think it was hatred that finally wrecked him. The pressure from society was too great. There will always be people as eccentric as Jiakai whose internal world is unspeakably bitter. They simply cannot bear the pressure and go insane. Alcohol saved Jiakai from the depths and fires of his suffering.

For many years, Jiakai was single. It was not until the '70s, from a stroke of good fortune, that he found Xiao Luo. Xiao Luo was from Tong County. She was unaffected and broad-minded, otherwise she could not have put up with Jiakai. Not long before they were to be married, Jiakai came to see me, swearing that he was not good enough for Little Luo. With all his strength he urged me to be the groom in his stead. I lost my temper and just about chased him out of my house. How could I carry off another man's beauty? The angrier I got, the more Jiakai laughed.

Jiakai finally moved into the Luo family compound in Tong County, making him a minor landowner. With the liberal reforms of the 1980s, he sobered up enough to stagger along and catch up with the times. Perhaps because of his unhappy past when he never had enough clothes to wear, he became a tailor. After a while, he was the number one authority on pants in Tong County. He then pressed his forces into Beijing where he opened a tailor shop and served as a consultant for a clothing emporium. But he still continued to eat his liquor and curse the heavens.

I left the country for more than ten years and lost contact

with Jiakai, though news of him dripped back to me from friends and family. I only knew that Xiao Luo, in answer to Deng Xiaoping's appeal, opened her own factory and got rich. Jiakai stopped making pants and stayed home eating alcohol.

I think it was during one of those years when Xiao Luo was still a worker in the county-run factory that she stole some little fish from the damaged, substandard bins, which were then passed through Jiakai's hands to his friends. This wasn't a big deal, comparable to me taking a few bricks home to use as pillows when I was a construction worker—it was the way things were done. But then a movement nobody expected surfaced and all factories were investigated for the loss of foreign currency reserves. The situation frightened Xiao Luo to tears. Jiakai ran all over the city like a madman, searching for those little fish. At the same time this was going on, the government was looking into rumors of counterrevolutionary activity. The fish Jiakai had given me I passed on to my girlfriend and cousins, who gave them to other people. After changing hands several times, those little fish were about as difficult to track down as counterrevolutionaries. I worked as hard as nine cows and two tigers, but could only retrieve two of them. Jiakai was distraught for a very long time.

Many years later, from the boundless ocean of people, the little fish swam back to him.

UNCLE LIU

I

UNCLE LIU IS ACTUALLY THE stepfather of my ex-wife, Shao Fei, but I've been calling him "Uncle Liu" for almost twenty years now. Fortunately, he has never taken me to task for it. When I was pursuing Shao Fei, he was wooing my future mother-in-law—we were like two planets entering a galaxy at the same time.

In March of 2001, Uncle Liu and his wife came to the U.S. to visit relatives. I hadn't seen him for several years. His back was even more hunched, his hair and beard were completely white, and most of his teeth had fallen out. But he was ever the optimist: as long there was drink, life was wonderful. He couldn't keep still and was either planting and watering vegetables in the backyard, or riding a bicycle around town and coming home with old vegetables loaded on his back. I had lived in the U.S. for a long time but didn't know that the larger stores, like the farmers' markets in Beijing, sold off piles of old vegetables at a discount.

Uncle Liu loved to fish, so we went to a nearby stream to take a look. He clasped his hands behind his back, like a senior officer taking a riverside stroll, and smiled broadly, clearly forming a plan in his mind. We bought a fishing license, prepared a fishing pole, and early one morning I drove him out. On the first cast he broke the line; after the second cast, the fishing pole was pulled out of his hands. Once he changed to a thicker line, disaster struck the foolish American carp as they were pulled one after another to our dining table. Uncle Liu had a limited number of teeth and could only eat a little soft food. As soon as he had some strong spirits in his belly, his eyes shone, and after a few drinks, he began to tell stories.

His grandfather was a Guangdong tea grower. A Russian merchant wanted to start a tea plantation in the Caucasus to bring Chinese tea to Russia. He traveled to Guangdong and recruited seven Chinese people, including Uncle Liu's grandfather. These troops were hustled off to the Caucasus, but they did not adjust well to the unfamiliar climate and all caught malaria. Two of them died, four fled, and Uncle Liu's grandfather almost breathed his last. The Russian merchant brought him to Moscow for treatment. With the change in climate he was soon his old self again. The wheel of fortune began to turn in his favor and as the tea plantation prospered. The tea his grandfather planted even won a gold medal at the Paris Exhibition. This drew the tsar's covetous eye so he took over the tea plantation. Soon after this new pot of tea had brewed, the October Revolution swept through. The tsar ascended to Heaven and the tea plantation fell under the control of the Soviet authorities. The new functionary drained a cup of the Chinese tea in one gulp and Uncle Liu's grandfather was awarded the Red Flag Medal of Merit.

The Liu family tree has another honor to its credit. Uncle Liu's grandfather's eldest son moved to Russia at the age of eight. He was later sent to St. Petersburg to study. When the guns of the October Revolution started to fire, he was an ordinary student with neither party nor faction affiliations.

Yet he eventually became the representative of China to the Third International. The Chinese Communist Party had not yet been established at that time. Mao Zedong was still in Changsha waiting to make a name for himself. A step ahead of them, this young man devoted himself to saving Chinese workers trapped in Russia. He met with Lenin, who wrote a letter clearing the necessary channels for their repatriation. As he escorted the Chinese laborers to China, he was detained by Zhang Zuolin in Harbin. Fortunately, the Chinese military attaché in Russia vouched for him and he was released. He stayed in Harbin where he worked for the Central and Eastern Railway Office and quickly rose to a supervisory position. He rode the train of revolution on the border between two languages, whose terminus was his compilation of *A Russian-Chinese Dictionary*.

His grandfather's youngest son, Uncle Liu's father, did not have such a glorious career. After graduating from high school, he was kept close to his father's side, raising horses, planting crops, and taking care of the tea fields. When he was nineteen, he fell in love with the daughter of the Georgian manager of the plantation. In spite of her parents' opposition, the two married in secret.

Uncle Liu's full name is Liu Jie. He was born in Batumi in 1923. He is half Georgian. This was an advantage as it made him a natural professor of Russian, but it was also a disadvantage, for during that extraordinary period called the Cultural Revolution, it made him a natural "Soviet revisionist special agent."

When he was six, Liu Jie's family moved to Harbin. His father found a job at the Central and Eastern Railway Office. After the September 18 Incident when the Japanese invaded Manchuria, they moved to Beijing. His father first worked in the Imperial Palace copying old Russian documents, then became a professor of Russian at Dongbei University when it moved into the interior. After the July 7 Incident of 1937, he was no longer able to teach, and left for Lanzhou. Liu Jie and his classmates saved the wounded, risking their lives in the thick of death. His mother was worried for him so she scraped together enough funds for him to go find his father. He turned fifteen that year, not yet graduated from middle school.

One summer, my whole family drove to a campground at Lake Tahoe in the Sierra Nevada Mountains. Clouds piled on top of mountain peaks, the mist-covered waters of the lake stretched out endlessly, and the redwood trees towered into the sky. They say that this is the clearest mountain lake in the U.S.—so clear that you can see the water plants on the lakebed. At dusk, we built a campfire by the tents to ward off the bursts of winter winds. Uncle Liu was in charge of the fire. He gathered branches and pinecones for fuel, then boiled water and barbecued some meat. As the night deepened, my mother-in-law, wife, and daughter all went to sleep. Only Uncle Liu and I were left sitting by the fire, sharing his broad-mouthed bottle of vodka. The pinecones we threw into the fire emitted white smoke and crackled as they quickly burned to ashes and embers. We watched the ever-changing and inexhaustible patterns of the flames without tiring.

Liu Jie traveled from place to place searching for his father. Once he found him, he started working as an apprentice at an auto repair shop. His father went away often, purchasing furs for trading companies. At that time, the route taken by transport vehicles providing military assistance to the Soviets passed from Kazakhstan and Xinjiang to Lanzhou and Xi'an, and then on to Chongqing. These caravans traveled in groups of two to three hundred vehicles, with machine guns mounted on those in the front. Rest stops were established along the route to provide food, lodging, translators, and local guides. Liu Jie took to them like a fish to water, following these caravans from east to west and west to east. When Russian soldiers, far from their homes, heard his pure Russian accent, we could only imagine how delighted they must have been.

On his way to Anxi to see his father, he was diagnosed with an appendicitis. The health worker for the Soviet caravan only had painkillers. In Anxi, the pain grew even more intense. Anxi is a tumbledown little county seat with only one street and no pharmacy or doctor. Sometimes planes on their way to Lanzhou would stop there to refuel. The stationmaster promised that as soon as an airplane arrived, even if it was a fighter plane, he would get the pilot to bring Liu Jie to Lanzhou. Liu Jie lay still for days, staring at the sky. When the pain abated somewhat, he'd walk along the street. He endured three months of intense suffering before catching a bus to Lanzhou.

Lanzhou had just been through an intense bombing campaign—ruins and corpses were everywhere, and the hospital had no beds. Liu Jie found some members of the Soviet air force that he knew from playing volleyball. They led him to a Russian health worker who scratched his head, saying that he understood in theory how to remove an appendix, but he had never actually done it and wouldn't do it unless they could find an experienced nurse. An old nurse was found, but she didn't speak Russian, so they recruited Liu Jie's aunt's coworker, a Chinese woman who understood Russian, to translate. The operation was carried out in the operating room of the bombed hospital. The moment he was cut open,

the translator fainted, and Liu Jie had to translate himself.
But this quack couldn't find the appendix no matter how
hard he tried, poking and prodding as the incision got bigger
and bigger. Furthermore, the morphine they used was bought
on the black market and must have been watered down as it
quickly lost its power. Liu Jie was in unbearable agony, cursing constantly. He refused to translate any more, hoping for
death to end the pain. But the surgeon finally found his appendix, and somehow, with the assistance of the old nurse,
managed to remove it and sew him back up. The wound
ached for two years before it finally healed completely.

In the autumn of that year, Liu Jie returned to Anxi, but
his father had already left. The Dragon King Temple, which
was seven li away from the county seat, had been changed
into a Russian caravan rest stop where several of his father's
students worked. It was just around the time of the Mid-
Autumn Festival, and some students invited Liu Jie over for
dinner. After serving Liu Jie wine and meat, his hosts urged
him to spend the night as it was late, but he stubbornly
insisted on returning to the county seat. It was very cold outside. The students found a sheepskin coat for him to wear.
The moon glowed brightly and the wasteland grasses rustled.
A path led him to a river that passed noisily under a wooden
bridge. Halfway across the bridge, he was startled by a pair of
luminous green eyes, clearly those of a lone wolf that also
wanted to cross the river. He had heard old people say that
you should never turn and run when you meet a wolf, otherwise the wolf will lunge at your neck from behind. Liu Jie suddenly thought of a way out of this predicament. He took off
his sheepskin coat, put it back on inside out, then leaped forward while barking like a Tibetan dog. The wolf backed up
two paces, then turned and fled with his tail between his legs.

2

UNCLE LIU LIKED DRINKING AS much as he enjoyed life
itself. If he didn't have half a catty of hard liquor during the
day, he wouldn't make it. By American standards, he should
have been sent to an alcoholism treatment center long ago.
During a three-year famine, he had a hard time finding liquor
and drank a number of substitutes, including alcohol-based
perfumes. Since marrying my former mother-in-law, he's been
barred from drinking. But if those on the top have their poli-
cies, those on the bottom have their own counter-policies,
and Uncle Liu hid his liquor away in soy sauce and vinegar
bottles that he would drink from while cooking. But how
long could he keep this up? Let him drink, let drunkenness
dissolve his unhappiness.

Liu Jie only completed one year of high school, then
tested into the education department at Gansu Academy (the
precursor of Lanzhou University). Because he was young and
dashing, he was constantly surrounded by female classmates.
He liked sports and was the captain of the school volleyball
team. At one game, after a ferocious spike, he realized that the
gold ring he wore on his little finger was missing. The referee
signaled a time out and all the team members got down on
their hands and knees in the yellow dirt to search for it, but
they couldn't find it. When he returned to the dormitory, he
told his inquisitive friends the story behind the ring. . . .

Because Lanzhou was a distribution center for Soviet
military assistance, it became one of the prime targets for
Japanese bombing raids. In those days, Lanzhou's alarm systems were quite thorough. Not long after a Japanese plane
took off from Yuncheng in Shanxi, the preparatory alert was
given; as soon as it had passed Pingliang, they issued the for-

mal alert; and when the plane was closing in, they gave the emergency alert.

One night at three in the morning, the preparatory alert sounded. Liu Jie followed the crowds out of the city gates and up into the mountain. Most of the air raid shelters were halfway up the mountain—a few caves three or four meters deep with no supports. He lay outside one cave. There was no wind, just a few wisps of cloud; the stars were huge and dazzling. At dawn, the alarm announced incoming planes like a cock welcoming the new day. The sky began to pale as the anti-aircraft guns fired beautiful varicolored tracers. He had just retreated into the air-raid shelter when the ground shook violently. Everything went black—the cave had collapsed. The sounds of sobbing and shouting blended together. Relying on his survival instincts, he furiously dug forward with his hands. The sounds of crying stopped as the air became thinner. He struck another pair of hands, a girl's, and on her left hand was a gold ring. He and the girl from the next cave had dug through. In the dark, they held tightly to each other, whispering softly.

When he woke up, Liu Jie was lying outside the air raid shelters while rescue workers looked for survivors in the piles of earth. He saw a girl of fifteen or sixteen sitting near him staring off into space. She was wearing a pink jacket and a green skirt, and had a long, thick braid and a gold ring on her finger. Their gazes crossed. Was that you? The girl happily leaped to her feet. Her name was Xiao Fang. She had been on her way with her aunt to get engaged.

"Why do you want to be engaged? Why don't you just marry me?" Liu Jie asked half-joking.

She replied, "That'd be fine with me. Coming so close to

death has bound us together. I wasn't very happy with the match, anyway."

Gunpowder smoke filled the air, people cried and shouted all around them, the stretcher brigade carried the wounded away. They paid no attention to this scene, but clasped each other tightly, swearing eternal devotion. Xiao Fang's even bangs covered her face, her eyes were full of tears. She gave out a little laugh and said, "My aunt is still hiding in that trench over there. I should go bring her out."

The trench was not far, at most four or five hundred meters. Xiao Fang disappeared inside as a second wave of bombers flew over. A bomb landed squarely in the trench, smoke billowed into the air. Liu Jie rushed over like a madman, searching through the heap until he found a small hand with a gold ring. He buried the hand and placed the gold ring on his own hand.

Ah, that's enough of that, Uncle Liu sighed. We were in the back courtyard of the Sudwerk bar drinking beer. This was the only bar in our town that brewed beer. There weren't many customers yet. The light of the setting sun streamed past the umbrella over the table and fell on Uncle Liu's face. My gym was next-door, and whenever I went to workout when Uncle Lin was in town, I brought him here to drink beer and read the paper. He and his wife were going back to Beijing the next day. The sound of someone playing jazz piano was being broadcast into the courtyard.

Uncle Liu met Lin Lin when he was a university freshman. She was a refugee student from Fujian. The student dormitory used to be the testing hall for the old provincial examinations. Its stone steps were worn, the corridor's pillars faded, and its tall pear trees rustled in the wind. From Liu Jie's room, a small passageway led to the medical school's morgue. The paper covering both sides of the passageway windows was tattered, and he was always coming face to face with newly arrived corpses. Lin Lin was a student in the medical school. She was often in the morgue alone, dissecting corpses. Once, she was sitting on a high stool, holding on to a body while examining it, when she accidentally struck who knows what tendon and the corpse's arm embraced her. She screamed for help, which is how they met.

It was spring and the pear trees were in full bloom, dazzling the eyes. They were both each other's first love. Cavorting on Gaolan Mountain, they talked about the state of the world, and looked forward to the future.

In 1943, when they were about to graduate, both of them were busy preparing for their final exams. For a while they did not see each other. It was only when he ran into Lin Lin's classmate one day that Liu Jie discovered she was seriously ill. He rushed to the hospital. Lin Lin had contracted acute pneumonia and had a high fever. He had her sent to the best hospital in Lanzhou and tried to find the best doctor for her. Her fever burned for a full month. Her body seemed to gradually disappear within her clothes. She fell into a coma for three days, but finally woke up in Liu Jie's embrace.

"I want to move," Lin Lin mumbled.

"Move where?" Liu Jie asked in surprise.

"To Gaolan Mountain."

At midnight, she breathed her last in Liu Jie's arms. The doctor on duty had her body sent to the morgue. Holding Lin Lin, he crossed the hospital's dim flower garden. An old man opened the door of the morgue. Liu Jie put her body on the table. He was unwilling to leave her. Later, the old man assumed Liu Jie had already left, and with a click, he locked the door. Liu Jie just sat in the dark holding Lin Lin's hand until dawn.

In accordance with Lin Lin's instructions, he buried her on Gaolan Mountain.

The piano piece came to an end. Tables were filling up, the sound of conversations grew louder. Uncle Liu fell silent. He peered ahead as if trying to see through the fog of sixty years. I noticed a small tear stop on his left cheek.

Every evening after Lin Lin died, Liu Jie could only get to sleep after drinking a bottle of hard liquor. After he graduated, he found an assignment at a newly established carpet mill in Qilihe, but he could find no pleasure or motivation in anything he did. One night, in his dormitory room, facing the bright moon outside his window, he raised a gun to his head and pulled the trigger. The bullet was a dud. Not fated to die that night, he threw the gun out the window.

3

As I DROVE US BACK from Lake Tahoe, the winding mountain roads made me jumpy. A piece by the French composer Erik Satie played on the tape deck. Sitting by my side, Uncle Liu slept, his head swaying back and forth, occasionally bumping against the window. He tightly clasped an antique black-and-white video camera. Uncle Liu could loosely be considered a video enthusiast since no matter where he went, he was always holding a video camera to his eye. This was one of his ways of observing things. I joked that whatever he saw when he went outdoors was always a secondhand black-and-white landscape. Regardless of the success or failure of his filming, he admirably threw aside all the tapes he filled, seldom bothering to look at them again—a truly aristocratic attitude.

Sometimes I wondered if this Uncle Liu and the Liu Jie of all those years ago were the same person. Who was telling whose story? Listening to his stories, it didn't sound like he was talking about the past. It was more like the past was talking through him. In a dream as brief as life, yet as long and drawn out, Liu Jie woke him up. Uncle Liu cleared his throat, clutched his video camera, and gave me a vital tip: Before you make these turns, tap the brake a little, then step on the gas lightly; the most important thing is to not brake hard while you are turning.

Before entering the university, Liu Jie was a truck driver for two years, driving almost the whole of northwest China. At the time, he was not yet eighteen. If the truck broke down on the road, in the middle of nowhere, no village ahead of him and no shops behind, he would send his apprentice to hitch a ride back to Lanzhou to buy parts, a trip that took ten days to two weeks. Alone, he would take his shotgun into the mountains, live off of what he could find, and at night sleep beside a campfire.

Once, after driving to Binzhou, Liu Jie drank and gambled with a number of other truck drivers. They were playing showhand, and the stakes were getting higher and higher. In the last hand, only Liu Jie and the boss of a trucking operation remained. He had no money left, but his cards were good, so he bet the keys to his truck. This truck was a rental, and of course when the cards were turned over the other man won. The owner of the truck company let Liu Jie keep driving the truck for an extra three months, which the winner agreed to. Liu Jie worked desperately. By hauling cargo for three months, he managed to earn enough money to buy the truck. "In those years," he told me, "the driver was master, hauling cargo or carrying passengers, doing whatever business was possible. With the exception of pilots, drivers made the most money."

And he almost did become a pilot. In the fall of 1944, he tested into the Shuangliu Air Force Academy at Chengdu, thanks in part to his unhappy first marriage. After Lin Lin's death, at the height of his sorrow, he had rushed into a marriage. But the couple did not get along. By flying an airplane, he could both fight the Japanese and flee married life. Liu Jie, though, suffered from vertigo. During the high altitude training, as he walked over a platform bridge, his legs turned to tofu. Japan surrendered and the civil war began, something far more fearsome than a broken marriage. He left the air force academy in a hurry.

First he wandered through the streets and alleys of Shanghai selling furs for half a year. Then he happened to meet up with an old colleague of his father who said the Chinese consulate in Tashkent needed a translator. So Liu Jie became an employee of the Tashkent consulate. Kuomintang political power was swaying like a tree in a storm. The ambassador to the Soviet Union snuck off, and the chargé d'affaires, who was also Liu Jie's cousin's husband, made Liu Jie head of the general affairs division of the Moscow consulate. At the end of 1948, not long after he had taken the position, Liu Jie was sent out on purchasing trips, making the rounds of cities like Stockholm and Paris.

I remember in the 1980s, after dinner before the plates and dishes had been cleared away, Uncle Liu used to tell us about his experiences in Europe. He said houses in Europe had spigots that, when turned on, released fresh beer and you could drink to your heart's content. At first I was somewhat suspicious, but then I thought: Well, Uncle Liu has been to a lot of places and seen a lot of things. He's probably right. How great it would be to not have to stand in line for beer! It was not until several years later, when I traveled to Europe myself, that I discovered this was nothing more than a drinker's fantasy.

In the fall of 1949, the Chinese Communist Party sent people to Moscow for talks with the Kuomintang consulate. At the conference table, Liu Jie, speaking on his own behalf, announced his revolt against the Kuomintang. He had expressed this plan to his cousin's husband before and urged him to return to China with him. But his cousin's husband said, "You are young and want to return home, this I can understand. But I have been abroad for a long time and no matter how good the Communist Party is to me, it would be too hard for me to change my old ways of thinking. Forget it, I would rather die a stranger in a strange land." So his cousin and her entire family, along with Old Qian, the previous head of the general affairs division and other officials, moved to London and Paris.

In the summer of 1992, my mother-in-law and Uncle Liu brought my daughter to Paris. Seeing the places he used to frequent stirred up all sorts of emotions. His cousin's husband had long since died, but his cousin was still living in the same house in the suburbs of Paris, silently knitting sweaters and the past together. The old head of general affairs, Old Qian, was still alive, but living in reduced circumstances in a tiny room in Chinatown. He frequently cooked up a batch of snacks and invited Uncle Liu and me over for drinks. He was in poor health, extremely thin, and his eyes bulged out. Listening to them talk about things that happened more than forty years ago made me feel that it had all happened in a world and an age far removed from my own. So-and-so has died, so-and-so is still living, so-and-so is seriously ill—their talk was like the calculations of fate, adding, subtracting, multiplying, and dividing . . . and what was left? The night before leaving Paris, Uncle Liu got very drunk and rushed into the bathroom in the middle of the night, where he cried for many hours.

In February 1950, Liu Jie returned to Beijing from Moscow. He didn't report to the Foreign Affairs Ministry, but asked a consultant who was in charge of hiring for the ministry to pass word on to Premier Zhou that Liu Jie didn't want to be a diplomat. He was twenty-seven years old. What happened in his life after that was not something he was willing to talk about, or if he spoke of it, he felt it had no point. I guess he was right, because after that time, the stories of all Chinese people are similar—a collective story, the story of a generation.

On the morning of the day he was to return to Beijing, Uncle Liu went down to the stream to go fishing one more time. At noon, I drove out to pick him up. For the first time ever, he did not catch a single fish. Seeming a little confused and at a loss, he put away his fishing rod and stood silently, hunched over by the side of the river. Old Guan, who went fishing, with him used to work for a central government committee. He later moved to Hong Kong and then retired in the U.S. He had never had much luck fishing, but this time he had caught seven hand-sized sunfish. I suggested they should be freed and that Uncle Liu should be the one to do it. He tilted the bucket. Scales flashed, the fish splashed back into the water. Uncle Liu turned around, chuckling.

New Directions Paperbooks—A Partial Listing

For a complete listing request free catalog from New Directions, 80 Eighth Avenue, New York 10011; or visit our website, www.ndpublishing.com

†Bilingual

Miroslav Krleža, *On the Edge of Reason*. NDP810.
Shimpei Kusano, *Asking Myself/Answering Myself*. NDP566.
Davide Lajolo, *An Absurd Vice*. NDP545.
P. Lal, ed., *Great Sanskrit Plays*. NDP142.
Tommaso Landolfi, *Gogol's Wife*. NDP155.
James Laughlin, *The Love Poems*, NDP865.
 Poems New and Selected. NDP857.
Comte de Lautréamont, *Maldoror*. NDP207.
D.H. Lawrence, *Quetzalcoatl*. NDP864.
Irving Layton, *Selected Poems*. NDP431.
Christine Lehner, *Expecting*. NDP572.
Siegfried Lenz, *The German Lesson*. NDP618.
Denise Levertov, *The Life Around Us*. NDP843.
 Selected Poems. NDP968.
 The Stream and the Sapphire. NDP844.
 This Great Unknowing. NDP910.
Li Ch'ing-Chao, *Complete Poems*. NDP492.
Li Po, *The Selected Poems*. NDP823.
Enrique Lihn, *The Dark Room*.† NDP452.
Clarice Lispector, *The Hour of the Star*. NDP733.
 Near to the Wild Heart. NDP698.
 Soulstorm. NDP671.
Luljeta Lleshanaku, *Fresco*. NDP941.
Federico García Lorca, *The Cricket Sings*.† NDP506.
 Five Plays. NDP506.
 In Search of Duende.† NDP858.
 Selected Letters. NDP557.
 Selected Poems.† NDP114.
Xavier de Maistre,*Voyage Around My Room*. NDP791.
Stéphane Mallarmé, *Mallarmé in Prose*. NDP904.
 Selected Poetry and Prose.† NDP529.
Oscar Mandel, *The Book of Elaborations*. NDP643.
Abby Mann, *Judgment at Nuremberg*. NDP950.
Javier Marías, *All Souls*. NDP905.
 A Heart So White. NDP937.
 Tomorrow in the Battle Think On Me. NDP923.
Bernadette Mayer, *A Bernadette Mayer Reader*. NDP739.
Michael McClure, *Rain Mirror*. NDP887.
Carson McCullers, *The Member of the Wedding*. NDP394.
Thomas Merton, *Bread in the Wilderness*. NDP840.
 Gandhi on Non-Violence. NDP197.
 New Seeds of Contemplation. NDP337.
 Thoughts on the East. NDP802.
Henri Michaux, *Ideograms in China*. NDP929.
 Selected Writings.† NDP263.
Henry Miller, *The Air-Conditioned Nightmare*. NDP587.
 The Henry Miller Reader. NDP269.
 Into the Heart of Life. NDP728.
Yukio Mishima, *Confessions of a Mask*. NDP253.
 Death in Midsummer. NDP215.
Frédéric Mistral, *The Memoirs*. NDP632.
Eugenio Montale, *Selected Poems*.† NDP193.
Paul Morand, *Fancy Goods* (tr. by Ezra Pound). NDP567.
Vladimir Nabokov, *Laughter in the Dark*. NDP729.
 Nikolai Gogol. NDP78.
 The Real Life of Sebastian Knight. NDP432.
Pablo Neruda, *The Captain's Verses*.† NDP345.
 Residence on Earth,† NDP340.
Robert Nichols, *Arrival*. NDP437.
Charles Olson, *Selected Writings*. NDP231.
Toby Olson, *Human Nature*. NDP897.
George Oppen, *Selected Poems*. NDP970.
Wilfred Owen, *Collected Poems*. NDP210.
José Pacheco, *Battles in the Desert*. NDP637.
Michael Palmer, *Codes Appearing*. NDP914.
 The Promises of Glass. NDP922.
Nicanor Parra, *Antipoems: New and Selected*. NDP603.
Boris Pasternak, *Safe Conduct*. NDP77.
Kenneth Patchen, *Memoirs of a Shy Pornographer*. NDP879.
Octavio Paz, *The Collected Poems*.† NDP719.
 Sunstone.† NDP735.
 A Tale of Two Gardens: Poems from India. NDP841.
Victor Pelevin, *Omon Ra*. NDP851.
 A Werewolf Problem in Central Russia. NDP959.
 The Yellow Arrow. NDP845.
Saint-John Perse, *Selected Poems*.† NDP547.
Po Chü-i, *The Selected Poems*. NDP880.
Ezra Pound, *ABC of Reading*. NDP89.
 Confucius.† NDP285.
 Confucius to Cummings. NDP126.

A Draft of XXX Cantos. NDP690.
The Pisan Cantos. NDP977.
Caradog Prichard, *One Moonlit Night*. NDP835.
Qian Zhongshu, *Fortress Besieged*. NDP966.
Raymond Queneau, *The Blue Flowers*. NDP595.
 Exercises in Style. NDP513.
Margaret Randall, *Part of the Solution*. NDP350.
Raja Rao, *Kanthapura*. NDP224.
Herbert Read, *The Green Child*. NDP208.
Kenneth Rexroth, *Classics Revisited*. NDP621.
 100 Poems from the Chinese. NDP192.
 Selected Poems. NDP581.
Rainer Maria Rilke, *Poems from the Book of Hours*.† NDP408.
 Possibility of Being, NDP436.
 Where Silence Reigns. NDP464.
Arthur Rimbaud, *Illuminations*.† NDP56.
 A Season in Hell & The Drunken Boat.† NDP97.
Edouard Roditi, *The Delights of Turkey*. NDP487.
Rodrigo Rey Rosa, *The Good Cripple*. NDP979.
Jerome Rothenberg, *A Book of Witness*. NDP955.
Ralf Rothmann, *Knife Edge*. NDP744.
Nayantara Sahgal, *Mistaken Identity*. NDP742.
Ihara Saikaku, *The Life of an Amorous Woman*. NDP270.
St. John of the Cross. *The Poems of St. John ...* † NDP341.
William Saroyan. *The Daring Young Man ...* NDP852.
Jean-Paul Sartre. *Nausea*. NDP82.
 The Wall (Intimacy). NDP272.
Delmore Schwartz, *In Dreams Begin Responsibilities*. NDP454.
 Screeno: Stories and Poems. NDP985.
Peter Dale Scott, *Coming to Jakarta*. NDP672.
W.G. Sebald, *The Emigrants*. NDP853.
 The Rings of Saturn. NDP881.
 Vertigo. NDP925.
Aharon Shabtai, *J'Accuse*. NDP957.
Hasan Shah, *The Dancing Girl*. NDP777.
Merchant-Prince Shattan, *Manimekhalaï*. NDP674.
Kazuko Shiraishi, *Let Those Who Appear*. NDP940.
C.H. Sisson, *Selected Poems*. NDP826.
Stevie Smith, *Collected Poems*. NDP562.
 Novel on Yellow Paper. NDP778.
Gary Snyder, *Look Out*. NDP949.
 Turtle Island. NDP306.
Gustaf Sobin, *Breaths' Burials*. NDP781.
Muriel Spark, *All the Stories of Muriel Spark*. NDP933.
 The Ghost Stories of Muriel Spark. NDP963.
 Memento Mori. NDP895.
Enid Starkie, *Arthur Rimbaud*. NDP254.
Stendhal, *Three Italian Chronicles*. NDP704.
Antonio Tabucchi, *Pereira Declares*. NDP848.
 Requiem: A Hallucination. NDP944.
Nathaniel Tarn, *Lyrics for the Bride of God*. NDP391.
Emma Tennant, *Strangers: A Family Romance*. NDP960.
Dylan Thomas, *A Child's Christmas in Wales*, NDP972.
 Selected Poems 1934-1952. NDP958.
Tian Wen: *A Chinese Book of Origins*.† NDP624.
Uwe Timm, *The Invention of Curried Sausage*. NDP854.
Charles Tomlinson, *Selected Poems*. NDP855.
Federico Tozzi, *Love in Vain*. NDP921.
Yuko Tsushima, *The Shooting Gallery*. NDP846.
Leonid Tsypkin, *Summer in Baden-Baden*. NDP962.
Tu Fu, *The Selected Poems*, NDP675.
Niccolò Tucci, *The Rain Came Last*. NDP688.
Dubravka Ugrešić, *The Museum of Unconditional ...* NDP932.
Paul Valéry, *Selected Writings*.† NDP184.
Elio Vittorini, *Conversations in Sicily*. NDP907.
Rosmarie Waldrop, *Blindsight*. NDP971.
Robert Penn Warren, *At Heaven's Gate*. NDP588.
Eliot Weinberger, *Karmic Traces*. NDP908.
Nathanael West, *Miss Lonelyhearts*. NDP125.
Tennessee Williams, *Cat on a Hot Tin Roof*. NDP398.
 The Glass Menagerie. NDP874.
 A Streetcar Named Desire. NDP501.
William Carlos Williams, *Asphodel ...* NDP794.
 Collected Poems: Volumes I & II. NDP730 & NDP731.
 Paterson: Revised Edition, NDP806.
Wisdom Books:
 St. Francis. NDP477.
 Taoists. NDP509.
 The Wisdom of the Desert (Edited by Merton). NDP295.
 Zen Masters. NDP415.

For a complete listing request free catalog from New Directions, 80 Eighth Avenue New York 10011; or go visit our website, www.ndpublishing.com

†Bilingual